DEER:
Sporting Answers

RECENT BOOKS BY RICHARD PRIOR

The Roe Deer – Conservation of a Native Species,
(Swan Hill Press), 1995.

Roe Deer – Management and Stalking,
(Swan Hill Press), 2006 Edition.

Humble Pie, (Swan Hill Press), 2006.

Deer Watch, (Swan Hill Press), 2007 Edition.

DEER:
Sporting Answers

RICHARD PRIOR

Quiller

First published in the UK in 2010
by Quiller, an imprint of Quiller Publishing Ltd

British Library Cataloguing-in-Publication Data
A catalogue record for this book
is available from the British Library

ISBN 978 1 84689 077 2

Printed in China

Quiller

An imprint of Quiller Publishing Ltd
Wykey House, Wykey, Shrewsbury, SY4 1JA
Tel: 01939 261616 Fax: 01939 261606
E-mail: info@quillerbooks.com
Website: www.countrybooksdirect.com

Contents

Dedication

To all stalkers' wives, and especially my own, for
coping with one of the most inconvenient hobbies
which this country has to offer. Impossible catering;
dreadful hours; nasty smells in the kitchen – let alone
what goes on in the garage.
You are all marvellous.
Also a profound salute to the roe themselves: delicate,
utterly charming and totally baffling, who have kept
me on the edge of my high seat, as it were, for more
than half a century.

Foreword

by Tony Jackson, past Editor of *Shooting Times & Country Magazine*

Think deer, and particularly roe deer, and you think Richard Prior. Possibly, no probably, the world's leading expert on these delightful animals, Richard has dedicated his life to their management and welfare, not only roe, but also the five other species which adorn these Isles. His qualifications are rather more than impressive. For sixteen years he was employed by the Forestry Commission to study deer in Cranborne Chase; he then joined the Game Conservancy, as it then was, as Information Officer and Deer Consultant, has twice been awarded the prestigious Balfour-Browne Trophy for work with deer and has travelled abroad on numerous occasions, studying deer and their predators. He has written fourteen books on deer and for many years has been a regular and much appreciated contributor to *Shooting Times & Country Magazine*.

All this is by way of saying that here is a man who knows what he is talking about and who, regularly consulted by a wide audience, has always been willing and able to assist newcomers to deer stalking and management. I have been privileged to know Richard since the early 1960s when I first joined *Shooting Times & Country Magazine* as the lowest form of editorial life, and in more recent years have been privileged to work with him as the deer expert on Sporting Answers which I have edited for the magazine. It has been a fascinating task, for Richard has invariably been able to provide an answer for even the most esoteric enquiry and has seldom been stumped … or if he has, has always admitted to it!

Here, in this selection of his Sporting Answers, Richard has provided the reader with a valuable cross-section of deer-related information, all of which is based on questions from *Shooting Times & Country Magazine* readers. The range of enquiry is staggering and illustrates the astonishing depth of knowledge and information which the author has garnered over the years. Here, in this book, the novice or would-be stalker will find a valuable *potpourri* of facts and information assembled in a simple, easy to read form.

Fortunately, for the welfare of deer and the education of stalkers, Richard will, I hope, continue to produce Sporting Answers for many years to come. We cannot do without him!

1 Deer lore – Ancient and modern

Time out of mind deer have been entangled in our developing culture. One can picture primitive men with their weapons of stone pursuing the dauntingly vast Giant deer across the grassy plains which then extended south from Ireland. Their aspirations, and maybe their religious hopes, were painted on cave walls like those at Lascaux in France. Others I have seen, painted and still vivid, on a rocky overhang in Siberia. In our own country, red deer antlers were used as picks to dig the flint for tool-making by the skill of flint-knapping. That skill persisted into our own era with the demand for shaped flint as building material and for millions of gunflints for the Napoleonic musket, later for flintlock sporting guns, and rifles. With the growth of sophistication, a search for meat to survive became formalised into hunting – almost a royal prerogative after the Norman Conquest. This in turn generated the panoply of the chase and use of the language of venery, some words of which are quoted below; some archaic, some still in use.

The surprising thing is that in spite of this long association, we are only beginning to know a bit more of the way our six species of deer live their lives. As the need for humane control and the popularity of woodland deer stalking grows, this in turn leads to a refreshing flow of queries through the pages of *Shooting Times & Country Magazine*, by e-mail and phone, and of course whenever a group of deer enthusiasts get together.

Questions on bygone days

Why was Saint Hubert chosen as the patron saint of sport? I think he went hunting on a Sunday and never went hunting again. Is that true? If so, he seems a bit unsuitable.

True in part. The original patron saint of hunting was St Eustace, a Roman commander named Placidus during the reign of Trajan, who, while hunting near Tivoli in Italy, was confronted by a stag with a glowing crucifix between his antlers. His place was taken by St Hubert who was supposed to be a prince of Aquitaine in the seventh century. Legend has it that while out hunting in the Ardennes one Good Friday he was brought to his knees by the sight of a stag with a crucifix hanging between its antlers and a voice threatening damnation if he did not repent. A life of good works followed among the pagans of the Ardennes, but he did not forsake hunting entirely, giving game to the poor. He was appointed Bishop of Maastricht and later canonised. But that is only one of the many versions! Compared with our somewhat nebulous St George he has a reasonable place in history.

His name is perpetuated in the Belgian town of St Hubert, where the Saint's Day is celebrated on the third of November, and in the existence of St Hubert Clubs in a number of countries. I vividly remember my initiation long ago into the St Hubertus Order in Austria, the Grand Master or whatever in full fig of loden garments and eagles' feather-decorated floppy hat. I was presented with a silver *bruch* or fir twig in celebration of my shooting a very modest *gams geisse* or female chamois. The St Hubert Club of Great Britain was founded in 1953 to foster good sportsmanship and the encouragement of better practice in the pursuit and management of game. They were pioneers in the regulated training of stalkers in the UK.

Reading an old book on hunting, I came across the word Hemule *referring to some sort of deer. Can you tell me what it might have been?*

A *hemule* was the old term in venery, or hunting lore, for a three-year-old roebuck. Medieval hunting had its own language, much of it deriving from Norman French. While he was Deputy Surveyor of the New Forest, the late Arthur Cadman felt that a revival of some of these would improve the respect which we had for fallow deer, for example referring to a third-year fallow buck as a *sore*. Some of these old terms are listed below:

Some Medieval Terms of Venery[1]

Species	Age	Names
Red stag	1st year	Calf; veel
	2nd year	Knobber; broacher; brocket
	3rd year	Spayard; brock
	4th year	Staggard
	5th year	Great stag; great soar
	6th year +	Hart
Red hind	1st year	Calf
	2nd year	Brocket's sister; hearse
	3rd year	Biche

[1] Extracted from Whitehead, GK, *Hunting & Stalking the Deer in Britain Throughout the Ages*, Batsford.

Species	Age	Names
Fallow buck	1st year	Fawn
	2nd year	Pricket; teg
	3rd year	Sorrel
	4th year	Sore; soar
	5th year	Bareback; buck of the first head
	6th year	Great buck
Roebuck	1st year	Kid
	2nd year	Gazelle; gyrle; girl
	3rd year	Hemule
	5th year	Fair roebuck

Other terms which you may come across:

Antlers –	the *attire of a stag*
Antlerless stag –	*hummel* or *nott stag* (West Country)
Lying in cover –	a red stag is *harboured*
	a fallow buck is *lodged*
	a roebuck is *bedded*
Hurdling –	skinning and cutting up a roe
A group of roe –	*a bevy*
The roe rut –	*bokeying* (I rather like that idea!)
Deer droppings –	*fewmets*; *crotties*.

You seem to use the word kid for the young of roe deer. I would spell the word for a young roe 'kit' (after the German 'kitz') rather than 'kid'. Would you agree? I'm not so sure about that 'kid/kit' issue. In German the word 'kitz' means 'roe fawn' – not 'kid' (child); it is exclusively used for roe. Similarly, in English only the roe fawn is called 'kid' – and it is a coincidence that it is the same word for 'child', but I don't think it is supposed to mean 'child'. I believe it comes straight from the German term and should therefore be spelled 'kit'. I have seen it spelled like that – but I fear I completely forgot where, so I cannot prove it.

So far as the first is concerned, it depends which language one is speaking. I am in England when I use the word kid. It's a perfectly ordinary English word, more often applied to goats. I prefer the word *fawn* which actually is incorrect as applied to roe deer. The medieval terms of venery, which had a strong Norman French derivations, used kid for the young of roe. I always used *fawn* until my publishers and others descended on me from a great height.

Savernake Forest was a Royal Forest from Norman times. It was largely an open heath, scrub and park-like landscape until the eighteenth century or so. The Saxon charters for the area describe really extensive hedges (haga, septa), running for literally miles, punctuated by occasional gates or stiles which serve as location points in the charters. These features, whatever they were for, have some resemblance to later deer parks, and, if fallow deer had been present in Saxon times, could have served an intended or incidental function of protecting and moderating the movements of deer (for hunting, trapping, etc.).

I would be interested to learn whether you think these vast long hedges, mentioned in the charters, could serve any purpose with respect to roe deer, or whether you have heard of management for this species in Saxon times.

Your scholarship will be able to trace the connection between *haga* and the medieval *deer hayes*. These were hedges laid out to assist the driving of deer into toils (nets) or enclosures where they could be slaughtered with the weapons then available. See *Encyclopedia of Deer*, GK Whitehead, Swan Hill Press, 1993, page 58. There was even a Royal Appointment – The Yeoman of the Toils – at one time who would have been responsible for producing either deer caught up for hunting or to furnish the royal table.

Current thought is that fallow were brought in by the Normans and would not have been present in Saxon times though new discoveries at Fishbourne suggest the Romans did import them but these deer may not have survived the Dark Ages. Roe were relatively numerous, but were not highly regarded, being deprived of protection under the Forest Law in the fourteenth century. Red deer are the likeliest species involved if, indeed, this was the reason for the hedges. If they ran for miles, then it may have had more connection with improving the hunting than for producing meat.

It is unlikely that the Saxons would have done more than hunt roe for meat and certainly would not have enclosed them. There are plenty of roe and red deer bones in Saxon digs, but no fallow have so far been found.

I am a beginner in the stalking business, and am trying to learn the jargon. Some of it is confusing – what, for example, is 'pronking'? It doesn't seem to be in any dictionary. Can you help?

Deer stalkers do seem to wrap up their talk with some esoteric terms, some of them coming from the Middle Ages. '*Pronking*' is a very descriptive term for the gait of a fallow deer bouncing away, all four legs in the air. According to a Dutch friend it comes (via South Africa where it is common behaviour in the Thomson Gazelle) from the Dutch verb *pronken* which means 'to show off'.

The different deer species move in quite individual ways. Red deer walk, trot, canter and gallop rather like horses. Fallow, when they are not pronking, walk and trot and may gallop after the first alarm. Sika deer, too, may bounce a few times, often looking back to see what has alarmed them, but then move more like red deer.

Roe at leisure have a very cow-hocked look but when alarmed break into a graceful bounding run, interrupted at intervals by a space-consuming leap.

Muntjac skulk, head-down, when pottering about, but they also scuttle with considerable speed, when they can resemble a small pig.

All species cat jump over surprisingly high obstacles, and they can also creep under fences.

When you have watched deer for a time, you get a good idea of the species involved by the way they move.

There used to be a sport called roe baiting. I can't believe that it had any similarity to bull baiting, or indeed hope not, so what was it? Had it anything to do with winter feeding, like they do with chamois in the Alps?

Fortunately roe baiting was not one of the cruel sports of our ancestors, but a way of outwitting a buck by lying in ambush on one of his known tracks while one hound was released into his favourite haunt. The ambusher, hearing the hound give tongue, had to guess the escape route of the buck and run to a suitable firing point before his quarry arrived. The main advocates of this, John Sobieski and Charles Edward Stuart (both claiming links with the royal families of Poland and Scotland) lived for many years on the romantic and picturesque island of Eilean Aigas on the River Beauly in the early part of the nineteenth century. A scarce book, *Lays of the Deer Forest*, describes their rather idyllic life and sport in what was then wild and remote country. With the somewhat inefficient weapons of their day, should a roe be wounded they thought nothing of pursuing it over days with a relay of hounds.

While I was sitting on top of a lofty and snow-covered high seat, two fallow emerged, one poor young buck, which paid the price, followed by an older white buck. Looked at through the scope, he had too much presence to shoot. I admired him as he went his way. Are there many white fallow about, and are there legends about them?

There is something special about a white buck, though they are often called 'Judas deer' because they reveal the presence of others. Most wild fallow herds have a few specimens.

Some stalkers, like you, admire and spare them but where night-poaching is rife the lights pick them up, so their numbers vary. In one area there was an outbreak of illegal dogging at night which changed the herd from common-coloured with a few black and odd white to mainly black because coursing lurchers went for anything with a white belly.

They are not albino, their eye colour being normal. Fawns start life a rich cream colour which gradually fades to white over the next one to four years.

In their book *Fallow Deer,* Donald and Norma Chapman link the popularity of *The White Hart* as a pub name to King Richard II, who adopted a white hart emblem on his badge. Technically hart refers to a red stag, but heraldry has merged hart and buck over the centuries.

We have a lot of public houses up here named White Hart. *Where did these originate and what is a white hart?*

Your second question is easier to answer than the first. A hart in the old language of hunting is a mature red stag. White red deer are known in a number of parks and at least one park herd, at Zleby near Prague, is all this colour. Occasionally a pure white specimen turns up in the wild which in some areas was considered a prime trophy, but in others, very bad luck to kill. So a white hart is that curiosity, a white red deer. Those I have seen were true albinos, but were poor specimens and appeared, besides their odd-looking eyes, to be deaf.

Kenneth Whitehead, in his *Encyclopedia of Deer*, stated that the origin of calling pubs *The White Hart* started at Ringwood in Dorset. On 11 January 1506, King Henry VII, with a posse of notables, hunted a white stag locally which appears to have been released for the purpose. It was taken after a good chase but at the ladies' request was spared, fitted with a golden collar and released to live a life of retirement in a park. This is also supposed to explain why pub signs often display a collared stag. An older story claims that where the deer (stag or buck) on a pub sign has a crown and chain round its neck it refers to a legend, as reported by Aristotle, that Diomedes consecrated a white hart to the goddess Diana and placed a collar of gold round its neck.

Another story relates to the village of King Stag in Dorset. A 'beautiful and goodly White Hart' which had previously given good sport, and had as a result been 'proclaimed' – that is, protected, was chased and killed by the royal bailiff, de la Lynde. This so infuriated King Henry III that he laid on the area a tax called White Hart Silver. It was paid regularly until late in the sixteenth century.

White Hart signs these days, and even some full-sized effigies on the pub roof, may display either a stag or a fallow buck, or the body of one and the antlers of the other! Some pubs are named *The Bald-faced Deer*. This is a reference to some strains of red deer which have a white blaze down the nose, like a horse.

In the north, and especially in the Highlands, to kill a white hind was generally considered likely to result in ill-fortune or even death for the shooter. Curiously enough the same superstition does not seem to attach to white fallow bucks, although in the Austrian Tyrol to shoot a white gams (chamois) is regarded as dreadfully unlucky.

General deer questions

Everywhere I go there are parties of deer out in the fields, which one never used to see. Why is this? Have the deer changed their habits, or are there just a lot more of them?

It isn't only in this country that fields are being used by deer. You only have to drive across northern France to see the same – small groups of roe miles out in the open – that is if you dare take your eyes off the traffic!

Like many other problems with wildlife, there is more than one answer to your query. One simple reason in this country is the widespread removal of hedges, giving wider views over the landscape. The deer are easier to spot. Also, studies of so-called 'field roe' abroad show that they are more likely to form sizeable winter groups in fields of more than about twenty-five hectares, realising that distance from cover adds to safety.

Deer population density does also have an important influence. Wherever I have seen roe behaving in this way there has always been over-browsing in any neighbouring woodland. Unlike cattle, which can cope with large quantities of lush vegetation such as grass, digestion in roe demands high-value food which is provided by the leaves, twigs and buds of the hedgerows and copses which are their natural habitat. A shortage of browse drives them out on to the fields, where they prefer to select the seed-leaves (cotyledons) of weed and crop seedlings or otherwise to subsist on crop residues and less nutritious grazing.

Numbers of roe and fallow deer did increase materially in the post-war years, partly fuelled by a huge increase in forestry replanting which provided food and cover. As those plantations grew up, the undergrowth on which the deer lived became shaded out, so an increased population of both species, faced with shortage of feed, especially in winter, were forced out on the fields. Nowadays roe have a definite sporting value which fallow do not share, so their numbers in particular have increased.

15

Are all young deer spotted? If they are, is this because they all trace back to a common ancestor?

All the deer we have in Britain have spotted young, and I suspect this is a characteristic which is shared with most if not all deer species. The reason is likely to be a practical question of survival of the fittest. That is, all new-born deer have to rely on immobility and concealment to avoid predators. A brown coat splashed with white tones blends in perfectly with the sun and shadows in a woodland or moorland environment. In addition, newborn deer seem to lack much body scent, another defence against predators.

Deer are widely distributed through the world with the exception of Central and South Africa. If, as is likely, they stem from a common ancestor this must have been a long way back. Fossil proto-deer had various antler-

A 'bald-faced' stag.

like projections but these do not appear to have been shed annually. We have no way of knowing whether the young were spotted, but camouflage was just as important for the young then as now.

They keep promising us a hard winter and I would like to help the local roe and fallow deer in the woods here if we get snow. I have the offer of some hay – would it be a good idea to buy some now while it is still cheap? Should I just make a stack for them to pull at, or does it need to be spread?

A small stack might be successful, properly protected from the weather, provided you do it early in the autumn. I have to say that hay is not the best thing to feed hungry deer. Once it is on the ground it gets wet and trodden so more gets spoiled than eaten. In addition, a change of diet from woody browse such as bramble to hay needs a couple of weeks before they can digest the new food properly because the bugs in a deer's rumen will not be right at first to break it down, and they need time to adapt. A deer can starve with a full stomach because of this.

It would be better to supplement their normal food by cutting ivy (an old hedgerow thorn often bears a heavy load) or some fir branches for them to browse once the snow arrives.

I shot a doe in this year's cull and noticed some very unusual deformities to her feet. These I photographed and showed to a person on the BDS stand at the West Country Fair at Shepton Mallet. I forget what he actually said it was called, but I think it was along the lines of 'Persian Slipper'? Apparently it is quite rare, and only a few cases are found each year. He advised that I should have had them preserved for study but unfortunately I was unaware of this at the time of shooting and had already buried them.

The beast was an old girl, her teeth were well worn down and she weighed twenty-nine pounds clean (chiller), she had a lot of ticks and lice in her groin area and a few bare patches on her head and neck. She had two well grown and fit looking youngsters with her (buck and doe) and was also carrying twins, on inspection of the gralloch.

Yes, this condition, where one or more of the cleaves become grossly elongated, is known as Turkish or Persian slipper. Nobody knows the cause, though some viral connection has been suggested. One might assume that it would be the result of living in a totally soft environment, such as a peat bog, but that is not the case. Some years ago several cases among sika were reported from Lundy Island, which is certainly not boggy. There seems to be no particular district where more examples are reported; on the other

This doe was suffering from elongated cleaves, a condition known as Turkish Slippers. The cause is not known.

hand, I am not aware of the condition occurring in red or fallow deer. Possibly there is some genetic influence. Age may be involved, but this again is uncertain. Mentions of it in the literature are very sparse. Not even Kenneth Whitehead's *Encyclopedia of Deer* mentions it. One of those splendid mysteries of deer biology which make our lives bearable!

Do deer eat ivy and yew? I thought they were both poisonous, but all the trees in my wood are stripped of ivy each winter as high as a deer can reach. The yew trees are browsed too and I think I saw a fallow buck chewing at a yew branch the other day. Will it die? What is eating them, if it isn't deer?

Yew, as all horse-owners know, is poisonous to equines and many other animals too. Deer are fortunate in possessing the ability to withstand its toxins to some extent. I have watched both fallow and roe browsing yew with no visible ill-effect. However, if a yew tree falls over, especially if this happens when the deer are hungry, they may gorge on it and in that case it may prove fatal. Slightly wilted foliage is more dangerous than when it is fresh. In the arctic winter of 1963 a big yew tree fell over in Cranborne Chase and seven fallow bucks were found dead in the vicinity. Some years ago fallow locally showed an anomaly of the liver which was apparently similar to cirrhosis in humans and was attributed to their having eaten yew over a period. In and out with other foodstuffs, they seem normally to take little harm from it. Deer do seem to like the taste of yew; they also, surprisingly, eat young laurel tips, but rhododendron is largely ignored.

The same does not apply to ivy, which is a valuable resource. If ivy is present it will be browsed for preference and one can get some idea of the species present by the height to which the leaves have been eaten, as well as indicating the browsing pressure on the habitat. If all the ivy has gone by February, you can be sure that any forest plantations in the area will be under pressure and unprotected plants are likely to suffer.

Is it really true that deer don't like sheep? There always seems to be some about on the hill to get in the way when I am stalking. In fact deer benefit from them as the normal semi-wild blackfaces act as all-too-efficient sentinels.

I agree with you that sheep are usually to be found and can be a nuisance when one is stalking on the open hill. A couple of sheep need to be nego-tiated round as carefully as if they were hinds. The deer certainly take notice when an old ewe runs off or gives that awful snort. In those conditions sheep are few and scattered. It is different on low ground and especially thinking about fallow and roe, rather than red deer.

Like most things in nature, several factors come into it: take the change from cattle farming to sheep – new fences have to replace old barbed wire which is easily slipped through by deer. Sheep fences usually consist of metre-high wire mesh plus one or two strands above which can be a serious barrier, if not a death-trap to deer trying to jump it. Shepherding involves the disturbance of daily visits accompanied by one or more sheepdogs. Not least, sheep at high density foul the ground. The noise and smell also appear to be repellent to deer while cattle seem to be tolerated. Fields grazed off by sheep are unlikely to attract deer until rain and regrowth have refreshed them.

Against this, if deer living in adjacent woodland are short of food, or just to confound the experts as they love to do, they will be seen out with the sheep and sharing their grazing.

Numbers of roe deer living out in the fields in winter often indicates overpopulation.

2 Mainly about roe behaviour

I f you try to be dogmatic about what roe can be expected to do at any particular moment, you are sure to be wrong. This is a highly successful animal which has survived and flourished by being almost infinitely adaptable, astonishing the onlooker at every turn.

We probably think of these deer as a woodland-loving species, almost monogamous and highly territorial, yet if conditions are better in the open they move out and become 'field roe', forming herds at least temporarily, because banding together appears to be a safer option there than living alone. In woodland the scents coming to their ultra-sensitive noses and the sounds in their radar-like ears are paramount, but in the fields they soon learn to use their eyes to spot even distant movement. If the mountains provide luscious feeding in spring and summer, but become snowbound later in the year, then they can migrate. And it is not just the Siberian species which has this ability, European roe have also been recorded making mass movements in response to harsh winter conditions, mainly in Eastern Europe. In Moldavia, just to be different, mass movement is not triggered by deep snow in winter but by the lack of available water in summer.

There are some fundamentals of roe biology which do help our understanding. For example their digestion is not so highly evolved as in some ruminants so roe need a comparatively nutritious diet, explaining their habit of browsing in preference to grazing on grass. Diet apart, getting to understand their way of life is made easier if you equate them, at least to some extent, with ourselves. The saying 'An Englishman's home is his castle' applies just as much to a roebuck's territory. Despite this, roe social life is dictated by the female; it is definitely a matriarchy. He is the one with the showy spikes on his antlers, but she leads.

Trying to get on terms with roe, it's best to think 'If I was a roebuck, what would I be doing this morning?' If it's a lovely spring morning, I might be patrolling the boundaries of my territory. Or exchanging the time of day with my next-door neighbour over the fence. (They do have friends.) On the other hand, a miserable cold sleety day finds him sheltering under the roe equivalent of a bus shelter. Occasionally you can catch him with his pants down – for example when he has been living safe and nearly unseen in standing corn. Then suddenly one day the combine rashers it all off, but it takes a few hours for him to realise that he is all in the open. He is like an old gentleman in the war whose club has been bombed; all his long-established routine demolished overnight.

Above all, he is an individual and incapable of conforming to any pre-set pattern. With mature bucks one gets amiable characters and belligerent ones. Among yearlings there are the bouncy, aggressive types and others who are too meek and self-effacing to make it worthwhile for the territorial buck to boot out. Recognising these traits is the bedrock of a successful stalker's knowledge, his passport to success.

Last September I think I saw a roe doe eating mushrooms. At least there were some in the field which I found had been nibbled when I went to look. Is this a normal part of roe diet?

There are plenty of references in the literature of roe eating mushrooms of various sorts. You will find an illustration of roe deer digging out fungi in JG Millais' classic *British Deer & their Horns*, published at the end of the nineteenth century. Curiously enough, in a lifetime of watching deer I have never actually caught one in the act, though I have been shown the small pits dug by roe in Denmark in search of some sort of fungus, exactly as drawn by Millais. Sadly, we do not have too many places where field mushrooms grow these days, but there are plenty of other sorts for the deer to find, so I don't think it is too common in my part of the world.

Arthur Cadman found that the New Forest sika deer had a preference for a false truffle called the Lycoperdon Nut which they would detect and dig up. Red deer are also known to eat fungi on occasion.

When I boiled out a roebuck's head last summer I found that there were two supplementary teeth in the upper jaw. Is this very rare?

These are rudimentary canine teeth, which do occur from time to time although they are not normally present in roe. Most stalkers don't look as carefully at the beasts they shoot as you do! Unless you look for them you can't know they are there! They may protrude less than a centimetre outside the gum and are usually rather loose in the sockets. There is a suspicion that quite often they are lost by the time the buck is two or three years old. If you look carefully at a collection of skulls a percentage are quite likely to have the sockets where these teeth once grew. It sounds as if yours are rather larger and better-seated than many examples. I think that it is more common in roe from fairly rich habitats and may affect 1 per cent of the population. They often fall out when the skull is boiled.

While out deer stalking in early July I culled a roebuck and when I gralloched the beast, the top of the heart was white with a lot of fat attached. Could this buck have had some sort of heart disease, and the top of the heart was white through lack of blood supply?

It appears that your buck had done himself well to judge by the deposition of fat round the heart. It is unlikely that this was anything more than a sign of good condition. Wild deer are normally very healthy and none of my reference books mention a record of heart disease. Lack of exercise and a far-from-natural diet make this much more likely among modern humans than roe deer! This chap had obviously been feeding himself up in preparation for the rut.

I shot a poorish roebuck the other day which when I skinned it was infested with maggots along its back. What are they, and should I ditch the carcass?

These are warble fly larvae, which are much more common on red deer. In this country they are only found north of the Scottish border. Eggs are laid on the legs, which hatch into larvae which migrate to the back, where they grow into the large, disgusting maggots which you found. Although very disfiguring, they do not affect the meat, as they lie directly under the skin. When due to hatch they tunnel through the skin, leaving holes which spoil it for tanning, and emerge as flies resembling a common housefly.

I enclose some photographs of a skull found in a local wood. No other remains were visible. The predominant species in the area are roe, fallow and the occasional muntjac. After much debate no one can make a positive identification. Is it a muntjac or maybe even a hermaphrodite roe?

First of all, it is a roe skull. As well as growing tusks in the upper jaw, muntjac have very large pits in front of the eye sockets which make identification of them easy. A fallow skull would be bigger.

Finding the lower jawbone would have been useful, but thanks to your excellent photos it is possible to make some deductions. The open central suture of the skull, just a wiggly line, shows that it was a young beast, which is confirmed by the teeth. The premolars are still milk teeth and the last molar (no. 2 of the permanent set) is newly erupted. The deer was therefore less than a year old and died in the late winter or early spring.

Obviously the long pedicles caused confusion. A small percentage of young male roe in good condition, as one would expect them to be in Hampshire, tend to grow very small antlers in their first winter, called 'fawn buttons'. These grow from December onwards, clean of velvet in late January and are shed in February before the typical 'first head' grows. This in turn will be frayed of velvet around May and shed again in late autumn.

On 31 March last, in a piece of mixed woodland we surprised a roe amongst the thickets. Both of us had it in sight a minute or so. It barked at us very gruffly before disappearing, still barking. We could not see any antlers, but neither of us noticed a tush on the still very creamy caudal patch. Is there such a thing as a roe hummel?

True roe hummels are very rare. In my life I have only ever seen two undoubted examples. This contrasts with red deer. Red hummels are not uncommon among Highland red stags and they are often successful in holding hinds against normally antlered opponents. It was always supposed that the condition was hereditary and that in consequence hummels should be shot as soon as possible, but experiments some years ago proved that this was not so.

In *Shooting Times & Country Magazine* of 16 September 1976 the celebrated roe enthusiast Henry Tegner reported that a true roe hummel had been shot in Northumberland. In 1992 Mr A Cohen shot a buck with very slight knobs on the skull not visible externally. He was very old and

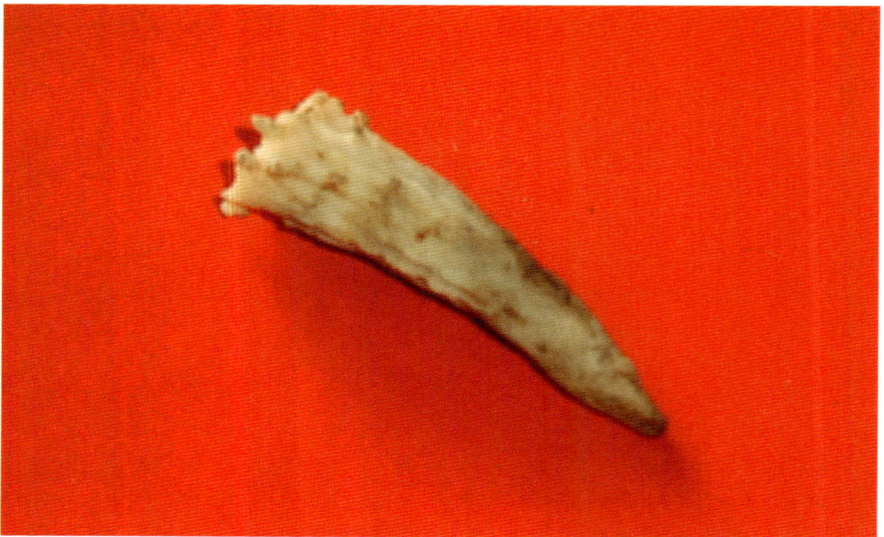

A cast fawn button. Some bucks grow short antlers in their first winter which are cast in February before the growth of the normal first head. At 40 mm this example is unusually long.

Although this buck had only flat plates of antler, it is not a true hummel. Note the well-developed pedicles, which might have born normal antlers in previous years. PHOTO: HUGH ROSE

had only one testicle. This must have been another true example regardless of the anomaly in his anatomy. Shortage of testosterone would not produce a hummel, but the exaggerated antler growth of a perruque.

I think it is quite possible that the buck you saw was indeed another hummel, though without at least a long and clear look through binoculars one cannot be sure that it was not an unusually aggressive doe whose anal tush was not plain to see.

Though roe deer literature often catalogues the disappearance and reintroduction of roe deer in England, I can find little reference to their fortunes in lowland Scotland, particularly the Forth/Clyde valley.

The late keeper on the estate in East Lothian where I stalk could remember the recolonisation of the estate by roe as recently as the 1940s. Was this entirely a result of southern spread from the Highlands, or was there northward spread from the Borders, or even reintroductions to the Lothian estates? Are there any reliable sources of records regarding the return of roe to this area?

This is a subject which has fascinated me, and I have done some research which is set out in my book *The Roe Deer – Conservation of a Native Species*

(Swan Hill) and GK Whitehead's tome *The Deer of Great Britain & Ireland* (1964); the situation can only be summarised here. It seems likely that roe were never eliminated completely from southern Scotland and the Border region. They were present near Hexham in the reign of George I (1714–27) and a pack of roe hounds was operating in Co. Durham in 1847. Some were released at Drumlanrig, Dumfriesshire in 1860, but JG Millais wrote in *British Deer & their Horns* (1897) that there were 'no roe, at least until recently, in either Berwickshire or Roxburghshire and that although some appeared in Selkirkshire around this time, they were killed off "as they interfered with the foxhounds"'. In 1892 Evans wrote 'it may also be seen from time to time in parts of East Lothian (the woods at Humbie and Salton, for example)'. They had reappeared in the neighbourhood of Berwick on Tweed by 1900.

I personally think that traces may well remain of the local, south-Scottish race, which is probably identical with the likely source of immigration from the English side of the Border. Analysis of DNA has so far failed to produce proof of the genetic origins of our roe, but it is possible that more may come from this quite soon.

Another semi-hummel which had pedicles but only buttons for antlers.

I know there are Siberian roe which are bigger than ours. Are they the same species? If they got that far, did they ever penetrate across to the American continent?

There are two species of roe – the European (*Capreolus capreolus*) and the Siberian (*Capreolus pygargus*). They are sufficiently near relations that hybrids do occasionally occur where they meet, on a line running very roughly north from the Caspian, but the cross is usually infertile. Siberian roe are bigger and longer in the leg but still resemble our own roe very closely.

Two groups of Siberian

roe are found, respectively west and east of Lake Baikal. Those of the Eastern community extending to Korea, often called Chinese or Tian Shan roe, are intermediate in size between the true Siberian and European types. At one time these were considered akin to the European roe and early authorities gave them sub-specific status as *Capreolus c. bedfordi*. Recent Russian research has proved the much more logical position that they are part of the *pygargus* group.

You can read more about Siberian roe in *Behavioural Ecology of Siberian and European Roe Deer* by A Danilkin, Chapman & Hall, 1996.

So far as I know, roe did not cross the land bridge to North America and no fossil remains have been found there to suggest it. One early writer referred to 'South American roe', but these were undoubtedly the Pampas deer (*Ozotoceros bezoarticus*) of Paraguay, Argentina and western Brazil which are roe-sized with rather similar antlers, but no relation.

Can one tell the sex or age of roe by its tracks (slots)?

Unlike the bigger deer species, there is no significant difference in weight or size between roebuck and doe. If you find a clear trace of several steps,

Two Siberian roe heads. Note the wide span, coronets which do not meet and a tendency to multi-point antlers.

you can sometimes see that a mature buck turns his 'toes' out slightly, while a doe prints hers more in a straight line, but mostly roe slots only indicate species, maturity and activity.

A newspaper item recently reported the appearance of a white roe – 'The first sighting in Scotland for more than a century'. In one of your books I seem to remember reading about white roe, so is this a little journalistic licence?

White or parti-coloured roe are a rarity but this is by no means the first example recorded in the Highlands 'for more than a century'. Many stalkers (and drinkers!) on Speyside will remember the skewbald buck which frequented a field just outside the Glanfarclas distillery a few years ago. It was eventually killed by a lorry and was fully mounted. I remember seeing it in this state at the Moy Game Fair. The photo I took at the time was reproduced in my book *The Roe Deer* (Swan Hill Press).

Other Scottish records have come from Fife, Argyll and Perthshire.

What on earth happens to my roe after the rut? Here, the rut usually tails off on about the tenth of August and suddenly I can't see anything but a few does wandering about. One of the old books spoke about a period of semi-migration or restlessness among roe at that time – is there anything in that? If there is, why don't I see other people's bucks suddenly appearing to replace mine?

I have read the book you refer to, and it may be true in some districts that some roe tend to change their ground, especially where something in the habitat changes, for example the harvest, a plague of flies, increased keepering activity where grouse are concerned, or with the approach of partridge shooting. In mountainous areas there is certainly a movement up or down the contours either to escape the flies (upwards) or in response to snow (downwards).

On the whole, I would suggest that your bucks are still where they were. The territorial males will have been exerting themselves with little time to feed and once the rut is over, until the beginning of September, they do stay very quiescent presumably recruiting their strength. One of the curiosities of roe digestion is that the absorptive surface of the rumen (stomach) through which much digested nutrient passes, is capable of increasing or decreasing. Thus at very active times of the deer year their metabolism increases in activity while at others, especially in winter weather, it decreases. This allows the beast to remain relatively inactive without losing significant body weight. I suspect that this post-rut period may be a time when this mechanism clicks in, explaining why one sees so little activity.

On the other hand, it may just be that the bracken just about hides every-thing! You can never be sure with roe.

The local roe have been a study of mine although I do not myself stalk. It appears that the question of yearlings being driven off in spring depends on whether the mother has been shot during the winter. My feeling is that it is only the orphans which are ejected.

It is always interesting to hear of other's experiences with roe, which are the most variable and adaptable of deer. The theory that yearlings are only driven off if the mother has been shot the previous winter is new to me and would make the subject of a worthwhile study. Such young bucks could be expected to be sub-standard, not the other way round. Are they driven out *because* they are slightly weaker, rather than the accepted theory that it is the strongest which get pushed out?

Speaking of buck yearlings, not the females, it has been observed in Holland that there is a progressive alienation from the mother through the early spring, and some examples of 'fagging' with an older buck before he becomes too territorially aggressive which may give a useful period of education to the youngster. Stronger yearlings, I was told there, will then be driven out by the older buck, but weaker specimens are too meek to attract his attention and remain as second-class citizens for another year.

How long do roe deer live? One of my bucks this year looked dreadful with a saggy back and stomach. Could he have been twenty years old, as somebody who knows a lot about deer has suggested?

The chances of your buck being aged twenty are remote. A long-term study of roe in France where the population was not controlled in any way gave the extreme age of bucks and does as fourteen and eighteen years respec-tively; the natural mortality of bucks increasing after the age of seven. Does breed less regularly after the age of twelve.

The signs of extreme age in a living deer are those you describe, plus a stiff gait and swollen joints due to arthritis, also in some cases silvering of the lower legs. Post mortem the teeth may be seen to be worn down or missing, the skull surface roughened, with the jaw and leg joints obviously arthritic. Antler growth is a notoriously bad guide to age, but really senile bucks are likely to produce thin or misformed spikes.

Of course in normal populations subject to management by culling, very few deer indeed survive for anything like this time, nor should they be allowed to. If old age sets in at seven years of age, this should be the cut-off point as far as it is possible to age deer sufficiently accurately in the field. Properly managed, on the basis of taking a significant percentage of the cull as yearlings, the *average* age is unlikely to be more than between two and three years.

Some of the roe I have shot have yellowish lumps in their lungs. Is this TB? Ought the carcasses to be buried?

Tuberculosis in deer is more often reported nowadays, and if you are suspicious about a carcass, get in touch with your local vet, who will probably advise you to take it to a Veterinary Investigation Centre. Roe are less affected than fallow. Even in the badger-infested TB 'hot spots' the disease has only been found in about 1 per cent of roe. The most usual centres of infection are the lymph glands, especially those lying behind the tongue (retropharyngeal) in the throat. I expect you will have been told how to examine these if you have attended a stalking course.

The lumps in the lungs of your roe are, however, much more likely to be caused by lungworm, a similar but not the same parasite as the one causing husk in calves. These can cause or contribute to loss of condition or even death in young roe up to eighteen months old or so. Lungworms are white threadworms which live in the air passages of the lungs and can cause partial blockage and consequent loss of condition or even contribute to early death. Reaction to their presence leads to the formation of yellowish, firm lumps, mostly on the edges of the lungs. Young deer seem most affected. Survivors of the first winter appear to tolerate them afterwards, though the lesions persist through life. Apart from the loss of condition, the edible quality of the venison is not affected.

The presence of heavy parasite burdens is often an indication of the deer population being too high, and in this case you should give serious thought to increasing the doe cull.

I've just had a phone call from a chap who has recently shot a roe with a 'clean' body weight, with head and legs on, of 25 kg (55 lbs). He was interested to know what the greatest recorded body weight for a roe is. Do you have any idea?

It depends what he means by 'clean'. To avoid misunderstandings, I distinguish 'clean' as the complete carcass, less rumen, intestines, liver and genital tract; 'quite clean' as clean, less heart, lungs and windpipe; and venison (dressed) as quite clean, less head and neck, lower limbs and skin. I have discovered that your correspondent means 'quite clean' which indicates that his buck had a live weight of about 33 kg (73 lbs).

The conversion factors for different methods of weighing are roughly as follows:

Live weight	100 per cent
Clean	82 per cent
Quite clean	76 per cent
Venison	55 per cent

I have a record of a buck which was claimed to weigh 40.59 kg (89½ lbs) live weight from Devon and one shot in Scotland in 1999 which weighed 32.2 kg (71 lbs) without feet or body contents, but with head, neck and skin on – estimated by a reliable source at about 43 kg (95 lbs) live weight. So this is not a record buck, but a very big one for all that. Curiously enough, some does are just as heavy. The largest one I have shot myself weighed 22.5 kg (49½ lbs) quite clean, or about 29.4 kg (65 lbs) live weight. Others as follows:

Wiltshire: 29 kg clean; Cumberland: 24 kg quite clean; Northumberland: 23.6 kg clean; Hampshire: 22.7 kg clean.

Do you have any knowledge of how long it takes for roe to move into an area after an old or dominant buck or doe has been culled or died? This assumes a fairly open boundary. Would it make a difference if the neighbouring land had little or no management taking place? This would be assuming that both pieces of land are roughly similar habitat.

The whole question of territoriality in buck and doe is a knotty one, depending to a great extent on the habitat and population pressures in the surrounding woodland. If one assumes that home range is the area occupied by an animal, but that territory is an actively defended area, most researchers state that the doe is only territorial around the time of the birth of her kids, and this territory may be at some distance from her normal home range. While a buck is territorial under most conditions in this country from March to October, this does not imply that he does not stray, either to test his neighbours' boundaries, to discover a better territory or in search of does in the rut. Indeed my feeling is that there is a degree of territorial breakdown in the later stages of the rut.

Research at Kalø in Denmark some years ago showed that a population could be shot out with little recolonisation, but that was in a district of very high shooting pressure and consequently low peripheral density. Conversely, if the surrounding land is under-shot there will certainly be a high element of influx. In the first place this is likely to be of young animals seeking living space, but where there are too many deer and heavy pressure on the available browse, it is more than possible that exploring mature bucks and does will find conditions more to their liking in their wanderings and decide to stay.

I had the stalking of a small wood in Dorset which was a magnet for big bucks. It was a mix of low hazel and bramble under oaks – perfect habitat for roe. By May each year these bucks had chased nearly all the yearlings away, and although I did not shoot many of them, those territories would be refilled by other mature animals from densely populated but inferior habitat round about.

As you know, in winter roe tend to congregate on the best feeding. In spring they may already 'have an eye' on a good location, and although it may be occupied then, if later a vacancy occurs there will be a scramble to get possession.

It's a bit like wild brown trout. Any particularly good lie is likely to hold one of the best local specimens. If that one is caught, it is astonishing how quickly the next in line has slid up to replace him.

Watching a small group of roe deer resting in the middle of a big downland field during one of the recent severe gales, I noticed that while three of them were understandably facing into the wind, the fourth was looking downwind. Are roe like wild geese, and post a sentry?

Unlike geese, deer rely more on their noses and hearing than on their eye-sight. While quick to spot movement, their vision is not really acute. When they lie down in what looks like a pretty inhospitable place, it usually turns out to be more sheltered *at ground level* than is at all obvious to us, some irregularity producing either a lee or a back-eddy. Three of your deer may have been benefiting from such local conditions, the other may have been out of it. There is, of course, added security in forming a group, but a single deer often chooses to lie so that it can watch downwind, trusting to scent to alert it to danger from the other direction.

While watching field-living roe in Poland I was told that these groups do indeed post what looks like a sentry, taking turns and using piles of bales as observation posts! On the other hand, it may just have been young deer playing 'King of the Castle' as lambs and fallow fawns do.

I have had a reliable report from Angus of a pair of roe apparently in full rut in May this year. This included the buck succeeding in mounting the doe. Is climate change affecting the reproductive cycle of roe, as it has of other wildlife?

There are no end of the wonders to be observed in the behaviour of roe.

All I can suppose is that in common with some other species, a post-partum female releases male-attractive pheromones. One thinks of the stoat and the muntjac for example, both of which habitually mate soon after the young are born. You wouldn't think that the buck had enough testosterone in him to induce mounting, but I don't doubt the report. He may not, I suppose, have achieved penetration.

Presumably the doe developed her speciality of delayed implantation in response to climatic conditions and one must assume that over time roe might be capable of changing back but I can't see it happening very quickly because (at least that's what one is told) implantation is controlled ultimately by day-length, not temperature. Beyond that, I don't know!

I thought that I read in the past that roe kids were born end of May beginning of June. I have just been reliably informed by one of our stalkers that a doe he has been watching that was heavily pregnant is now [7 May] as thin as a rake.

How can the seasons affect roe birth time, bearing in mind their delayed implantation? Is the timing more spread out than is often realised, or is there a regional variation?

To judge by the work which was done over many years at Chedington in west Dorset, the average fawning date for roe in the South of England is 22 May, but there are quite marked individual variations round this date. Even at Chedington, for four years (1968–72) the average date was 11 May.

Young deer need excellent camouflage while they are unable to escape from predators.

My own observations range from 30 April to late June. From time to time stalkers report obviously very young roe kids at other times of the year but I think these must be the rare occasions where the normal process of fertilisation and subsequent implantation has slipped a biological cog. Normally each stage of the reproductive process is determined basically by day-length, which of course does not change with alterations in climate; however there are some interesting variations through the range of roe, colder climates tending to be later. Quoting from Danilkin's *European and Siberian Roe Deer*, Hungary (14 April – 17 May) and Bulgaria (24 April – 5 June) report the earliest fawning dates, while Sweden (21 May – 3 July) and Russia (14 May – 11 July) are markedly later. Siberian roe are later again (Russian Far East 1 May – 25 July). This follows a rutting date for this species from July well into September. From this one could conclude that roe are capable of reacting to climate by slight adjustments to this reproductive cycle, but this is more likely to be a gradual process rather than marked variations from year to year.

Can you put me in touch with somebody who can supply roe deer for acclimatisation here in Ireland? It seems very suitable habitat with plenty of forestry and good grazing in between. We could build up a small population and then start letting stalking which eventually would help the rather stretched finances on the farm.

No. There are no roe deer in Ireland and it would be criminal to release them, no matter what the circumstances. They are not native to the island because they failed to pass from England at the end of the Ice Age. At the end of the nineteenth century they were introduced to Lissadell in Co. Sligo, and as you suggest, prospered and grew some very large trophies, some of which have been preserved. However, they were shot out between the wars *because of the damage they did to forestry*. The value of the timber industry to Ireland vastly outweighs any income which roe could generate, and the increase in establishment costs through having to protect new plantations would be completely unacceptable.

I have a stalking question, which I've been trying to research on the internet, but for which I couldn't yet find an answer; I wonder whether you could kindly direct me to where I could find an answer (if there is one). Also, I don't recall reading about it in your books.
   I'm sure you've heard this many times – do you believe the moon phases have any influence on roe deer behaviour, and is there any evidence/probability that stalking can be more effective under any particular moon (i.e. better avoid stalking under a full moon, better chances under a new moon, etc.)? I know that there

are many more factors that should be taken into account while stalking, but this is one that is intriguing me particularly.

You would have to go to one of my very early books to find the answer – it's in *The Roe Deer of Cranborne Chase* (OUP) pages 46–7. It's probably too old for you to find in a library (published in 1968), so I will give you the gist of it.

I was then stalking the same bit of dense south-country woodland every day, keeping records of what I saw for about three hours from first light and two hours before dark. This was for April to September 1962. There were significant peaks in numbers seen per outing in every month around the time of new moon, declining during the period of full moon (with the exception of a slight peak on 19 May). The greatest difference was for mid-June, between a peak of forty-five at 2 June and a trough on 23 June of five.

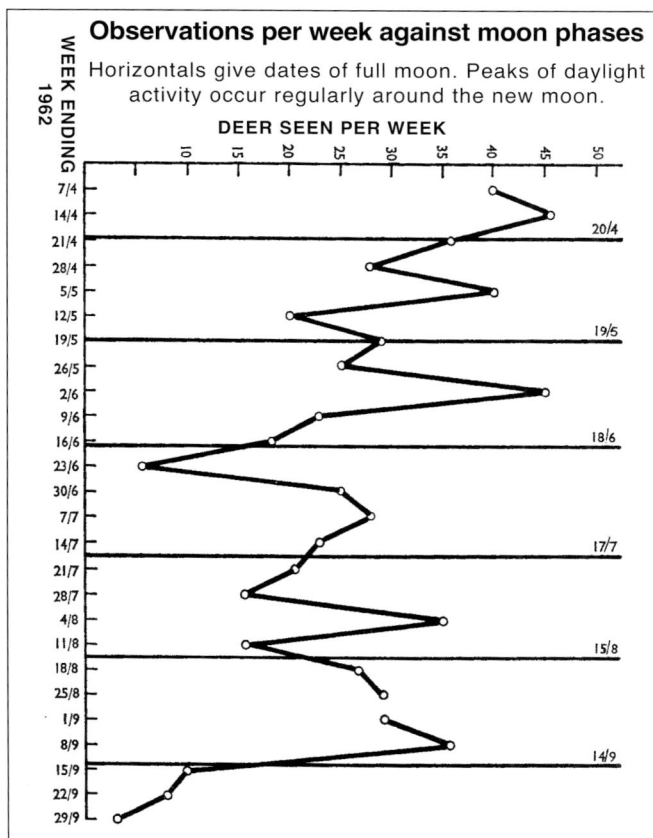

Observations per week against moon phases

Horizontals give dates of full moon. Peaks of daylight activity occur regularly around the new moon.

Observations of roe at dawn and dusk set against the phases of the moon. Obviously there is increased activity on moonlit nights.

35

So I do think that moon phase has an effect on numbers seen in this type of woodland in daylight, probably reflecting nocturnal activity when there is light enough to see reasonably. The same probably applies in the rut, when many stalkers have less success with calling during the full moon. Of course, as with everything to do with deer, it depends on many factors, not least their delightful inconsistency!

I have noticed that last year a roe doe on my grounds has produced twin bucks. These bucks have wintered well and are now almost out of velvet but the heads vary considerably (one very nice, one murder buck). Why is this? Is it possible that the doe has conceived two youngsters from different bucks to produce a genetically different fawn? It has been a very mild winter with no shortage of food in this area, so don't believe it was simply a case of one buck faring better than another.

Like all knotty deer problems, some guesses are needed! Roe does only have one oestrus, and on occasion they do mate with several bucks in quick succession late in the rut, probably to make sure of pregnancy, so a mix of sperm is technically possible. While feed, as you say, is important, another possibility for one fawn doing better than its twin might be that one had a greater birth weight than the other, so is more aggressive and thus getting a better share of the milk. Alternatively, one may have picked up a dose of lungworm affecting its general health and therefore antler growth.

If you decide to cull out the lesser buck, it would be interesting to see if its lungs show the typical signs of lungworm – thickened paler patches on the edges of the lungs. However, research has shown that the antlers grown by yearling bucks bear little relationship to those grown in later life. Culling decisions are better made according to body weight than by the size of a yearling's antlers.

We seem to be losing a lot of roe fawns each winter – mostly from January onwards. Some of them are obviously in poor condition, but others look OK though the carcass is often fairly far gone when they are found. Have we got a disease problem, or is it something to do with agricultural chemicals?

If on the whole you are losing fawns (kids) rather than adult deer, the finger points towards overpopulation rather than either disease or poisoning now that some of the most toxic sprays have been banned. Winter is the testing time when suitable feed may run very short and the young suffer, having fewer reserves. It is worth having a careful look at your hedges and in the woods to see how severely the undergrowth, ivy and lower branches have been browsed. If there isn't much left at this time of year then there are too many deer. Another sign is the formation of large groups of deer in the bigger fields, the so-called 'field roe' phenomenon. They go there because the woods can no longer support them but farm crops undiluted by woody browse make deer scour and they lose condition.

Lungworms, similar to but not the same as those causing husk in calves, are a factor in mortality among young roe deer and indicate that the population is too high. If you find a fairly fresh carcass is it worth looking at the margins of the lungs for lighter-coloured, rather hard patches. One can sometimes find the actual thread-like worms in the air passages of the lungs.

Competition from other deer – fallow in your area – can raise the browse line higher than the roe can reach.

The answer to all these signs is to increase your cull, but remembering all the time that the only way to reduce the breeding herd is by culling females.

Do you think roe in some areas are more predisposed to bark than others? I get the feeling that it is the does that do more of the barking than the bucks but I have no proof, just a feeling that when I am in their home the females give me more stick than males? What have you found?

A couple of stalkers called in this morning who confirmed my feeling that there were places where bucks seem to bark more than usual. This quite apart from the habit they have of barking more in the rut. My experience suggests that such places are often valleys where they may be responding to a local echo. From February onwards to the end of August bucks do bark aggressively which I assume to be part of a territorial display, all part of the business of avoiding physical contact by a variety of threat displays. If two bucks do have a fight, the victor is likely to bark loud and long.

With does I think the short bark they give is more in the nature of an enquiry, rather than aggression. They are certainly inclined to 'box' with their front feet, but I haven't heard a doe bark in connection with this. Both sexes when disturbed give the typical long-drawn 'Baagh – baagh – baagh' as they bounce away with targets fluffed out. I have never been sure of the purpose of this, as neighbouring deer outside the immediate group sometimes take no notice, any more than I understand the reason (purpose?) for the occasional click produced by the cleaves when they are running fast.

I was coming to the end of my stalk in northwest Hants this morning when I came across a young roe doe. I had seen her a couple of times before but never this close (thirty yards), but noticed something odd.

She was feeding quite happily oblivious to my presence when I noticed that when she had swallowed her mouthful and finished chewing she started to cough; it was loud enough for me to hear it and through my binoculars I could quite easily see her mouth opening and shutting and her flanks moving with the cough.

She is a small beast with the last vestiges of her winter coat visible, but was alert and not showing any signs of lameness or being stressed. She stopped coughing and moved into the crop (beans) a little further where she halted to carry on feeding. After another couple of mouthfuls she began to cough again, after this bout she moved well into the crop and out of my sight.

I was reluctant to shoot her until I could confirm that she has a serious problem. I think this animal may be suffering from a lungworm problem. It's the coughing that got me puzzled as I have never seen a roe cough and your books describe them as 'rarely heard to cough'.

I culled an adult roe doe and youngster from the same wood as this one lives in back in the winter and did not find or see any lung problems with those.

If it is lungworm, will the animal recover or will it eventually debilitate her to the point of killing her?

It is very unusual to hear roe cough, but the fact that your doe was still in partial winter coat in mid-June shows she was ill or debilitated in some way. Lungworm affects young roe and can weaken them to the point where they don't survive. Prevalence of the worm can indicate that the population of deer is too high. Mostly they recover and although the lesions (pale, thickened patches round the edges of the lungs) remain through life, it doesn't seem to affect them after, say, two years of age.

The decision on whether to cull a doe out of season on humanitarian grounds is difficult. If, when you see her next, she is skin and bones, it would probably be kinder to shoot her, but roe are very resilient and I think it likely that she will recover.

I enclose the skull and lower jaw of an ancient old gentleman I shot recently. This is exactly how I removed the lower jaw – only tissue and muscle holding it together. I think he was very old, it would seem from his body weight and his reaction to me while stalking him that his senility was due to his injury – amazing how he survived!

The old buck has many interesting points. Obviously from the slope to the coronets and his tooth wear, including the incisors, he is as old as you suspected. But looking at his teeth the fact that wear, though extreme, is similar on both sides suggests that the accident to his jaw happened comparatively recently. His knobbly, short antlers indicate debility, likely to be connected with age and a general lack of bodily activity last winter. He has not even had the strength to polish velvet off them.

To survive at all with a completely broken jaw only shows once more the amazing power these animals have to survive the most horrific injuries. However, he could not possibly chew the cud, so his term of life after the accident could only be measured in weeks, as his reserves cannot have been great in the first place. Poor chap. What caused such a fracture is anybody's guess. There are no signs of bullet strike. Assuming that you do not have gangs of hooligans chasing your deer at night with 4x4s, my guess is that he was hit by a car on the left-hand side of his head (there are signs of a longitudinal crack on that side, indicating a sideways blow, possibly by something jutting out, like a door mirror).

My partner in the east of England has found triple foetuses in several does, in the same locality over several seasons, and has seen a doe with what appear to be triplets. Do they have a genetic predisposition to throw triplets, being passed on in some areas, or is it the result of very good feeding? Suffolk being largely winter corn and rape, with coppiced woodland, what do you think? If it is basically food then we should get triplets in several high quality feed areas. But the Suffolk area does seem to have some of the best yielding agricultural land in the country from what I am told. What we surmise is that even if they carry to full term, protecting triplets from predators is probably too much to expect, unless the doe is lucky. Might get away with it with very low fox numbers, and no badgers.

We have solid research results which show clearly that body weight influences the fecundity of roe. Quoting work by Hewison and others in *The European Roe Deer: The Biology of Success*, Scandinavian University Press, 1998, it has been found that heavy does of all age classes are more likely to ovulate *and/or implant larger litters* than lighter does. In contrast, high population density decreases ovulation. So your partner's Suffolk roe are obviously benefiting from quality feed and habitat. It may be that the roe population is lower than, for example, in many parts of southern England. Possibly the predator situation is different as well. This slightly begs your question about a genetic tendency to throw triplets, just as some human families go in for twins. Dealing with a wild animal and one not commonly throwing triplets in any case, it would be extremely difficult to set up a project to study this, so in the present state of knowledge I would suggest that the underlying cause is good feeding with, as you suggest, good post-natal survival.

In a day's roe doe culling at the end of February there were several with dirty backsides. I also noticed a good buck with the same. One of the does was in very poor condition, but the others were fine. Is this something to be worrying about?

The normal diet of roe consists of a mixture of woody browse, buds, leaves and ground vegetation. In early spring most of the palatable browse in the woods and hedgerows is used up. One can tell this by the way ivy has been cleaned off trees and nothing much remains on the bramble stems but old and thorny leaves wherever they can reach. With the first weeks of spring deer are attracted to arable fields, taking advantage of highly nutritious seed leaves (cotyledons) as they push out of the ground, both cereal and weeds. Once the cereal leaves are ten centimetres (four inches) high they are less attractive, but until they have been sprayed off, deer continue to seek out the new weed shoots.

This change in diet from woody to sappy feed can upset roe digestion and produce scouring, as you have noticed, so that the white target and hind legs are fouled with faeces. This normally clears up as bramble and other shrubs come into bud. If it continues, it may be prudent to collect some droppings and ask a vet to examine them for parasitic worms.

Finding one emaciated doe without any obvious signs of the cause might be unrelated and could be the result of some injury or mishap, parasites or disease. If you notice more on your stalking ground, then more careful investigation is called for.

Have you had many reports this year of an unusual number of very small, poor roe fawns? In January I culled out three miserable specimens about the size they should have been in late summer. They were not orphans because they were accompanied by normal does. Their coats were scruffy with bare patches. I stalk in an area of downland where trophy quality is not special, but food should be adequate. I have seen others in the game dealer's.

Stalkers do report mini-roe like this from time to time, weighing little more than twice the weight of a hare even in the winter. It is likely that most of them have lost their mothers at an early age, but when just old enough to be able to browse and keep alive, though without a continued supply of milk or the habits of survival and safety which would be learned in the first few months of life.

Undersized and lacking the necessary knowledge of different food plants or of avoiding potential dangers, the chances of these mini-bucks or does living through even one winter are slim. You are right to have no hesitation in weeding them out as seen. They are unlikely to thrive or make good breeding stock.

Animals in poor condition tend to have severe infestations of lice (Damalinia) showing bald patches before the normal spring moult.

In your case, where they are obviously not orphans, one looks for another cause. The bare patches of skin indicate the presence of lice – always an indicator of poor condition. I would suggest they are probably picking up lungworms, or liver fluke of which the secondary host is a water snail. If you come across another, have a good look at the lungs for thickening at the edges, or for flukes in the bile ducts of the liver. Failing that – is it over-population in relation to the food supply?

I stalk roe in Hampshire, and have recently been shooting a lot of does who had no hair around their necks. Initially I thought this might be mange or some other skin condition as some does were quite thin and sickly, but as I continued the cull more and more healthy big does exhibited this condition around the neck. I'm aware they're shedding their winter coats just now but it strikes me as strange. Only the neck is hairless, can you shed any light please?

This is quite a common phenomenon with roe in the spring. They look scruffy because of their normal moult, but often before this starts they rub the hair on their necks until the white skin shows underneath. As you observed, some but not all of the worst cases are animals in poor condition.

The likely cause is a biting louse, *Damalinia* sp. which tends to congregate round the ears and then spreads down the neck, probably causing the animal intense irritation so that they scratch themselves with their hooves or rub against bushes. The heaviest infestations build up on young beasts and especially the least healthy. As the moult progresses, most of the lice are shed and a normal coat grows for the summer.

The biology of these lice is something of a mystery as, at least when I was finding out about them, no males had ever been found on a roe deer.

It is good practice to include any affected does in your cull as it is a good bet that many of them will be in poor health otherwise, possibly being affected by other parasites such as the sheep tick, or by accident or disease.

3 Natural history of other deer

or centuries we took our native wild deer for granted. Only those involved in formal stag hunting took a deep interest in them. From the Norman Conquest to the time of King John and later, deer were strictly preserved for the Royal Hunts, but from the Civil War onwards deer that were not 'imparked' were just a nuisance or a source of semi-illicit food for the peasantry. Within the parks which surrounded many of the great houses deer were regarded as an ornament and yet another reflection of the opulence of the landowner. One has only to look at a few of the books produced at the end of the nineteenth century, such as Walter Winans' *Deer Breeding for Fine Heads* to realise the significance these pampered herds represented in the social landmarks of the period.

However, it was not until the middle of the twentieth century that any serious attempt was made to study wild deer in a scientific manner. Frank Fraser Darling's *A Herd of Red Deer* was virtually the first. Interest in our five other species limped behind his pioneering work. Even now, with practically the whole country populated by one or several species we often have to look abroad for in-depth research. Enthusiasts concerned with fallow, roe and muntjac do benefit from basic monographs for each,[2] but sika and Chinese water deer have not so far had the same attention. This is stimulating! There are new facts to be discovered about our largest wild land mammals even now.

We found a muntjac fawn wandering about in the garden. I have put it in a cat basket and offered it some milk, which it hasn't drunk. I don't think it is new-born, so what ought one to do for it? There are lots of muntjac about, and they come into the garden and eat the tulips, but we are sorry for the little thing.

You must think what would become of the deer if you succeeded in rearing and taming it. Do you want it permanently in your garden? They are not easy to look after, and even more tulips would suffer. My advice is to put it back as quickly as you can, using the basket (open) as a shelter, and hope

---

[2] Chapman D and N, *Fallow Deer*, Dalton, 1975; Prior R, *The Roe Deer – Conservation of a Native Species*, Swan Hill, 1995; Smith-Jones C, *Muntjac – Managing an Alien Species*, Coch-y-Bonddu Books, 2004.

that the mother comes back. Wild things have to take their chance, and being objective, that is the best you can do for it. Keep it or release it, the odds on survival are much the same.

Are acorns poisonous to deer? Some of the oak trees locally have a very heavy crop of acorns this autumn. The fallow deer in a park I visit seem to like them without suffering any ill effects but I have often been told that farm stock could die from eating them. What is the true picture?

Acorns can prove fatal to cattle and horses if they eat too many, especially when green. Poisoning is thought to be caused by their high tannin content. Cases have also been reported of fallow deer being found dead with the rumen stuffed with acorns, but deer on the whole like a varied diet and are unlikely to poison themselves in this way if alternative food sources are available. Once dry and brown acorns provide a very valuable resource, lasting well into the thin months of winter if the crop is heavy. Especially with roebucks, which grow their antlers in the winter, a good mast year can have a marked effect on the average size of trophies the following season.

How did red deer and roe arrive on the Hebrides? Were they imported originally, or could they have swum?

Although there may have been human intervention in some cases, red deer

Deer are strong swimmers in spite of their slim legs.

and roe are quite powerful and bold swimmers, which is surprising considering their slim legs and feet. Fishermen quite often report seeing both species quite far from land. In spite of fierce tides between the islands, attempts to swim two or three miles would possibly succeed, though with inevitable cases of drowning.

When stalking on our ground in Lanarkshire I found several sets of red deer slots. Although none has been seen in our forest they are obviously present and it will only be a matter of time before they are seen/shot. The main forest is a block of 4500 acres of mainly sitka spruce and I wonder, if a colony of reds started living there, would they push the roe numbers down or would the roe resist such intrusions being a browser more than a grazer like the red?

The question of red–roe competition is debatable. One can't be too dogmatic about one species being exclusively grazers and the other browsers. Obviously if there are high numbers of the bigger species, they will use up all the available browse and the roe will suffer, but there are lots of places where woodland reds and roe co-exist quite happily at moderate densities. I have in fact seen a young roebuck following a stag around for whatever reason, and this has been noted by other writers. It can partly be a matter of the habitat being more suited to one than the other. If your block of conifer forest is getting into the pole stage with very little undergrowth, it would suit the reds quite well for cover between expeditions to the hill to forage, while the roe being more static might find it less amenable to their lifestyle. Sitka spruce is pretty unpalatable, so they have to rely mainly on what they can find along the rides.

Where I stalk in Somerset we have had muntjac off and on for several years in addition to a good roe population, but they don't seem to build up in numbers. Do the two species compete, or are the roe aggressive to the smaller deer?

While there are places where roe and muntjac co-exist, the penetration by muntjac into areas which are already well populated by roe has been slow and spasmodic, as you describe. Like lots of animal questions, the reasons are likely to be complex, but there are some possibilities which may apply to your ground:
- Muntjac are shorter in the leg than roe, and so the browse line in woods heavily populated by roe or fallow may be too high for them.
- While their habitat requirements are roughly similar, muntjac are very much at home in very thick undergrowth. If your woods are more open, they may make a better habitat for roe.

- Muntjac are very vulnerable to road accidents. Is there a trunk road nearby which they often attempt to cross?

I enclose a photo of a deer taken near Dunbar. Please confirm my identification as a sika. Has the species been reported from this area before, and if so, where did they come from?

I was interested to get your report of sika having penetrated as far as Dunbar, and to have a photo in confirmation is that much better! Fallow and sika have been confused sometimes, but the white hock glands and chevron on the face are diagnostic.

So far as I know, this is the first report of the species from your area.

As you probably realise, sika were first introduced about 1860 and were subsequently donated to several parks, from which they inevitably escaped. According to Kenneth Whitehead, the first sika to be brought to Scotland were introduced to Tulliallan in Fife about 1870, but the origin of your stag is more likely to have been Dawyck, Peebles where an escape from the park there in 1912 led to the formation of a stable colony in neighbouring woods. For many years there was only limited spread, but from about twenty years ago they began to push into new areas. Sightings were reported from the big Border woodlands and westwards, raising worries about possible hybridisation with the Galloway red deer. Sika like the habitat provided by large-scale commercial afforestation, and there is no barrier to them gradually penetrating the length of the Lammermuir Hills. They are in any case considerable wanderers, especially the young stags, as yours appears to be.

A report *The Distribution and Spread of Sika Deer in Scotland* by Suzanne Livingstone, Helen Senn and Josephine Pemberton was published in the BDS journal *Deer* in the Winter 2005–06 issue.

The jargon of deer stalking confuses me. Thinking about the fallow rut I thought that a major buck had a 'rutting stand' where he accumulates and herds as many does as he can. But now somebody who knows a lot about fallow says that they 'lek'. I thought that was something which blackcock do. He also talked about 'parallel walking'. What does he mean, and what am I supposed to see my fallow doing?

There are two fundamental mistakes in interpreting the behaviour of deer. One is to assume male dominance, the other is to think that they are going to behave the same under different circumstances. The notion of a stag or buck 'rounding up his harem' may be true sometimes, but ask yourself 'Why are the females there anyway?' It's because they want to mate, and consider for whatever reason that one male deer has more to offer than another. Sure, a stag can chase an individual hind, but while he does there is nothing to stop the rest from vanishing over the next hill! So a rutting stand is where one male sets out his stall and hopes to attract nubile does to him by making what noise and stink he can. On occasion fallow do 'lek' – that is, a number of bucks assemble and each marks out a small patch of ground where he demonstrates in the well-known way. Does are attracted to this assembly and then are free to choose one mate or another. It is indeed comparable to the blackcock's lek, with a number of males displaying, duly admired by an audience of females. Because of the proximity of one 'territory' to another, there is intense competition between bucks, but fighting is something to be avoided if possible, so they walk alongside one another in a very formal threat display known as 'parallel walking'. This too you can see in other species of animals and birds.

I have been stalking for nearly twenty years. This April I shot two sika stags, a pricket and one about three years old. The younger of the two stags had liver fluke. This is the first time I have seen this. Do wild deer shake this off?

The farmers in the area seem surprised that I have not come across this before as the disease is common in cattle. The stag with fluke was in no way run down or ill. I would be interested in your comments.

Liver fluke (*Fasciola hepatica*) is a leaf-shaped parasite found in the bile ducts. The secondary host from which deer pick it up is a water snail (*Limnaea truncatula*) so deer are more likely to become infested if they habitually graze in damp places, especially in the summer. Probably for this reason, some districts are worse than others, and the habits of individual deer are also a factor.

AM Dunn, in *Management & Diseases of Deer*, (ed. TL Alexander, Veterinary Deer Society, 1986), states that sika are hardly ever infected, which explains the fact that you have not come across it before. Fluke does seem to be tolerated to a marked extent by red and fallow deer although it is a significant cause of mortality or poor condition in roe, especially in some parts of western Scotland. Apart from looking for the actual parasites in the liver, the clinical signs are loss of weight, poor coat, soft faeces and soiled tail.

The fact that your pricket showed none of these seems to indicate that sika, in common with the larger deer species, are tolerant of fluke in the rare event of becoming infected.

Deer on the whole are very healthy. Although the larger species form herds, they do not huddle together as cattle do, nor are they confined at high density like domestic stock, with the exception of farmed deer. This helps to limit the spread of disease and parasites. They can, of course, contribute to spreading ticks and other organisms which may themselves carry diseases affecting farm stock. It was, however, significant that in the last dreadful outbreak of foot and mouth disease wild deer do not appear to have been involved. Scattered cases of bovine TB have been reported in deer from areas where there is a high incidence of this disease in badgers.

Even though transmissible disease is a rarity, stalkers should be informed about the clinical signs of all diseases likely to affect deer. Advice should be sought through your local veterinary surgeon, from the Game & Wildlife Conservation Trust or the British Deer Society, from whom specialist advice is obtainable. If you suspect TB or other notifiable disease, it must be reported immediately to the Divisional Veterinary Officer of Defra.

I am sending you the skull of a Chinese water deer buck. I would be grateful if you could tell me the age of this animal, and if possible explain the method of assessing age.

Your Chinese water deer is a fine mature specimen, qualifying for Gold under the CIC formula.

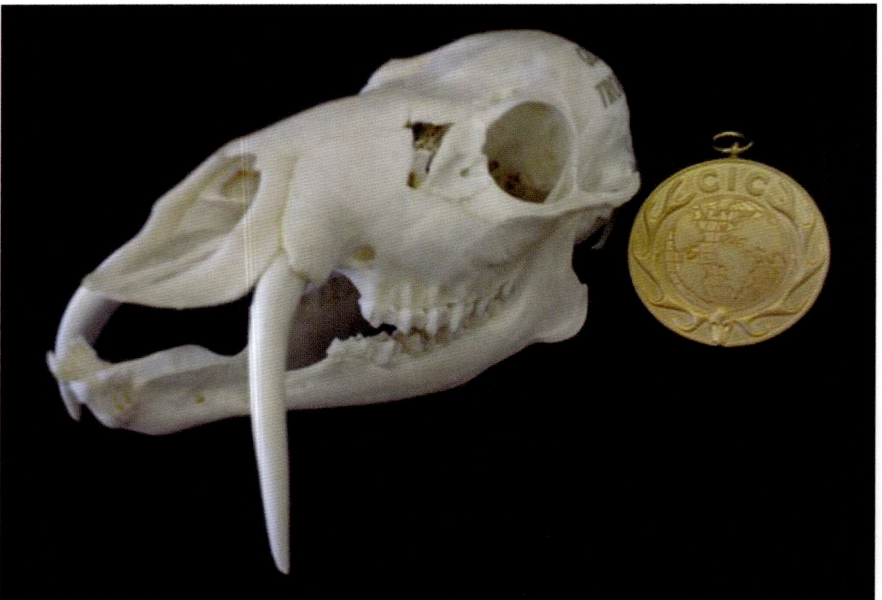

A Chinese water deer skull showing a fine pair of tusks.

So far as telling the age is concerned, I can only generalise as I have never had a great deal to do with this species. Looking at the molars and premolars, they are half worn and well embedded in the jaw, which indicates at least middle age. One should relate this to the life span of the species. I have no information on this. One would expect a relatively small deer to be old at seven to ten years.

I have learned from roe that one can be deceived by only looking at tooth wear because much depends on the nature of the food supply and the abrasive qualities of the soil. Deer from sandy areas wear their teeth much more than they do, for example, in south-country chalk country.

If you have kept the lower jaw one can tell more by looking at the anchorage of the chewing muscles at the angle of the jaw. These start quite flat but slowly the pull of the muscles induces the formation of ridges, on both the outer and inner sides.

If I were looking at a roe, I would also feel the thickness of bone over the eye socket and the smoothness or roughness of the frontal bones. Older animals are thicker and rougher respectively. Unfortunately pedicles aren't much to go by in Chinese deer! In other species they become thicker and shorter, tending to slope outwards at the join between pedicle and antler. One bit of evidence which is preserved in your specimen is the septum between the nostrils. In young animals this is cartilaginous, but slowly becomes ossified through life. Your buck shows a well-ossified septum, probably indicating late middle age or more.

I have volunteered to assist the BDS in counting deer in my area and when I attended the BASC Northern branch show I informed them that I had seen a buck muntjac on the land where I stalk. However, I was informed this was not likely as they were not yet so far north. I have stalking rights in Co. Durham, bordering the North Yorkshire area. On Saturday, 2 April I was with my future son-in-law on a farm close to Durham, ten miles from the city, when we disturbed a buck muntjac. It ran through low crops, about one foot high, with only its head showing and we are certain of what we saw. Can you give me a definitive answer as to where these deer are resident in this country, because I know I saw a muntjac.

The spread of muntjac from their core area in the East Midlands has been steady but irregular. There appears to be some interaction between muntjac and roe, so that colonisation is slowed where incursive muntjac encounter a fully stocked roe population. Also there has been the possibility that a semi-tropical species would be limited in its northern spread by harsher winters. In Bedfordshire many died in 1963, the foundation year of BDS and a memorably hard winter.

Small isolated communities have become established, it is assumed through relocation, though the release of muntjac in new areas is now quite rightly illegal.

The latest information, apart from the vital distribution maps produced by BDS, is Charles Smith-Jones' excellent book *Muntjac – Managing an Alien Species*, (published by Coch-y-Bonddu Books). The distribution shown there, although diagrammatic, clearly indicates that there are muntjac well north of the Humber although colonisation is not continuous. So your report of the species on the Co. Durham border is interesting, rather than unbelievable.

We have a few red deer here as well as the roe, and one roebuck appears to like to tag along after our resident stag. I know there are interactions between them where a stretch of woodland is occupied by more than one sort of deer, but do you ever see a definite association between one species of deer and another?

A mature red stag may tolerate the company of a 'squire' or 'fag' – a younger stag apparently acting as some sort of page and no doubt learning from a more experienced animal. Normally individuals of different species take little notice of one another although there are a few cases recorded of 'fagging' by roebucks with red stags. I remember seeing a stag in East Devon long ago pacing through the woods with a young buck pattering along behind him, but the explanation for this is obscure. That is the only example in my own experience. Between deer and domestic stock there is usually apathy or antipathy. Roe don't like sheep, possibly because they smell. Occasionally during the fallow rut a frustrated young buck takes to pursuing heifers round the fields, to their consternation, but this is hardly an association. One rather odd-headed stag in Hampshire took to doing the same thing, and also threw their feeding troughs about. The farmer didn't want him shot, so I put two rounds of 30-06 at his feet then sent my Labrador to drive him off. The dog came back after a while with such a look of disgust on his face at my missing such a large target that I had to laugh. On the whole, I would say your stag might be attracting a bit of hero-worship, but who is to know?

There are both fallow and sika in the local park, with some outliers as well. What is the chance of the two species mating, and would the offspring be fertile?

Hybrids between red deer and sika are all too common, in fact it has been suggested that most of the Highland red deer now have a trace at least of sika blood. Red and sika are, of course, from the same genus, *Cervus*, while fallow belong to the genus *Dama*. Therefore sika and fallow are too far apart genetically to make any crossing likely to produce viable young, let alone fertile hybrids.

Many years ago a male deer was shot in the circumstances you describe, on the outskirts of a park, which did display marked characteristics of both species. It had the diagnostic white spot on the hind leg and forehead chevron of sika, was spotted although winter-shot, but it had grown a palmated head very similar indeed to that of a fallow buck. Unfortunately, as so often happens in such cases, although material was saved and sent to a vet for analysis, somehow no results were ever forthcoming. One has to assume in the lack of evidence, that this was a pure sika which had (as is occasionally known) grown palmated antlers. In questions of this sort the solution is rarely out of the ordinary!

What is the correct definition of a 'royal'? Is it just a twelve-pointer stag, or are there more specific criteria? Does an imperial also have a specification?

To be correct, a true royal head must have twelve points, but in addition it must have 'all his rights', that is, brow, bay and tray (trez) on both sides and with the three crown points forming a cup deep enough to hold a glass of whisky! Lacking these, it may be a fine trophy, but remains a twelve-pointer. The term 'imperial' which is sometimes applied to fourteen-pointers has no valid history. It is supposed to be a fairly recent bit of one-upmanship. In the past some people have gone farther, calling an even ten-pointer a 'royal', a twenty-pointer a 'double-royal' and a thirty-pointer a 'triple-royal' – but never an 'imperial'!

If we get a really hard winter this time with lots of snow, will a great many deer die?

With the change of climate most of us have forgotten what a Christmas card winter can be like. Old stalkers will remember 1962–3 when we had snow in the south of England from Boxing Day to well into March. What was reported then was that a number of muntjac did die. With our vastly enlarged population of that species, it is perfectly possible that prolonged snowfall could result in a significant die-off of that species, and possibly Chinese water deer as well. This is something that is difficult to predict because so much has changed since then.

I was working on roe at that time and expected to see starving roe deer in all the woods, as in addition to the searing cold, everything they normally fed on was submerged under snow. However, two factors contributed to their survival. The crusted snow, on which they could walk, brought new levels of browse within their reach. Also the weight of snow led to many ivy-covered hedgerow trees falling over. Another material factor is that *where left undisturbed* the deer had the ability to reduce their daily need for food, either finding shelter or actually making forms for themselves in the deep snow from which they had no need to move, thus conserving their energy. If they were forced to flee from humans or dogs, vital reserves would soon be exhausted.

With winter rapidly coming I am looking at supplementing the food available to the deer in our woodland. Would it be OK to put out grain, carrots and turnips, or is there any better feed that I could put out?

To judge by the way they attack grain hoppers put out for pheasants, most deer must like wheat and benefit from it, so if you have a game shoot they are probably used to that, and could take grain from hoppers of the sort that trickle a small amount on to a lip. Too much might induce bloat. Open trough feeding would attract birds. If carrots or turnips are grown commercially in your area, they should do well. A vegetable packing plant will have rejects. The main thing is to feed a small amount at a time and start early so that they get used to what you give them. A rapid change of diet, especially when they are already hungry, leads to the deer gorging on feed they can't actually digest because the bugs in the rumen need to adapt to any change of diet, and this may take a couple of weeks. Feed regularly, otherwise a heap of useful material will rot or go mouldy.

In the long run, planting browse, such as willow, will provide a good cheap resource all year if you (or they) keep it well pruned.

I know there are white fallow, and rarely the occasional white colouring on other deer species. Is there such a thing as a white or albino Reeves' Muntjac? Has one ever been seen?

As you say, there are white fallow, and this is a natural colouring so that these animals have dark eyes and noses. True albinos lack all dark colour, so the eyes are red and the nose pink. Albinism can occur in any species but is often linked to poor vision and hearing. The white red deer which I have seen were albinos and certainly very poor specimens, though there is a strain of normal white red deer in European parks. In roe there seems to be a relationship between melanism (black) and albinism, with reports of individuals changing seasonally from one to the other extreme.

I do not know of another sighting of a white muntjac, but in Charles

A black roe. The tendency to melanism seems to be local. Occasionally a spotted, piebald or completely white deer is seen.

In muntjac colour variants are very rare. This mounted example in the Tring Museum is probably not Reeves' Muntjac, but another of the Eastern sub-species.

Smith-Jones' excellent book *Muntjac – Managing an Alien Species*, (Coch-y-Bonddu Books, 2004), he states: 'Although albinism and melanism have been recorded in muntjac, instances are rare compared to other deer.' As a postscript he pointed out that there is a white muntjac exhibited in the Rothschild Zoological Museum in Tring, together with a fine white roebuck.

Daphne Hills at NHM London was kind enough to give details of this animal:

> The white muntjac on display at Tring is a specimen of *Muntiacus muntjak*. There is no given locality but the specimen would have been collected between 1900 and 1930. A female white *Muntiacus muntjak* was previously displayed in the same case but is now in store. This specimen was collected by Lehman from Lukistan, North Borneo. I am not aware of any albino specimens of *Muntiacus reevesi* in the National Collections.

Muntiacus muntjak is, of course, the larger Indian species. Charles speculated whether the female might not be M. *muntjak* at all, but possibly M. *atherodes* (the Bornean yellow muntjac) which was not recognised as a separate species until the early 1980s.

Another sidelight on this was reported in the British Deer Society's journal *Deer* in summer 2009. Ian Pearce reported shooting what was described as a leucistic muntjac in Suffolk. The coat was grey – 'it had the look of a mountain hare in its winter coat'. Whether this greyish animal would have turned completely white with greater age is a possibility as is the case, for example, with horses.

Can deer catch bluetongue disease? What are the symptoms to watch out for if they do?

Bluetongue has been recorded in US white-tailed and other deer species, so there must be concern that our deer may become infected. The most obvious signs are eye and nasal discharge, drooling and ulceration of the mouth. In the white-tail, infected deer become lethargic and tend to lie down twenty-four to forty-eight hours after infection and generally die soon after, so the chances of their acting as a reservoir of the disease may be small.

Any suspicions that deer are affected must be reported quickly via the Defra helpline 08459 335577; they will give details of the nearest office. More details can be found at http://www.defra.gov.uk/animalh/diseases/notifiable/bluetongue/about/index

When, if ever, do deer actually sleep?

As you obviously suspect, the answer is rarely. Even when you see a deer curled up like a dog, to all appearances asleep, you will see that its ears are still turning, ready to receive any threatening or unusual sound. No doubt its nose is still ready to respond to any signal which the wind may bring. One could, perhaps, say that it is dozing but definitely not fully asleep and unconscious of its surroundings.

Nonetheless, occasions are on record of deer being found so deeply asleep that they have been taken for dead, only to go off like a scalded cat when touched. On one occasion a tractor driver cutting grass noticed a roe lying head on flank by the hedge. He drove his tractor and mower up to it, dismounted and assuming it was dead, caught hold of it before it woke up. Another's ears were seen to be twitching, his half-opened eyes were rolling and the buck was emitting small grunts, just like a Labrador dreaming in front of the fire. So they do sleep, but probably it's unusual indeed to catch one napping.

Sitting on a high seat in May, I was astonished to see a roe doe come past which was green. Had it been sprayed with something noxious, or how do you explain it?

Curiously enough, a friend phoned the other day with the answer. His dog ranged through a field of oil-seed rape in full flower – and came out bright green! Presumably this was a good coating of pollen. The dog is none the worse, and I think, to judge by the way so many roe have been living safely in deer-high rape since the start of the stalking season, that they are none the worse either.

We are just starting to see a few muntjac in the woods here during pheasant drives. They don't seem to be doing much harm so should we be doing anything about them? Will they compete with the roe which are still thin on the ground here and which we like to see?

Muntjac are serious pests of new coppice shoots and valued wild flowers, such as orchids and bluebells. In addition they can disrupt pheasant shooting if a buck starts running up and down a string of sewelling, to produce an uncontrolled flush. Where colonising muntjac encounter a fully stocked roe population, penetration of new ground is slow. In your area it is likely that both species will build up eventually.

Muntjac favour thicker undergrowth and make difficult targets for the

Muntjac can browse coppice growth and bluebells producing serious damage.

stalker as they rarely seem to stand still, unlike roe. I would certainly favour a strict culling policy to discourage successful colonisation. Some stalkers are reluctant to shoot muntjac does, knowing that they have no fixed breeding season, but this is the only way of reducing their capacity to reproduce. The species has no legal close season, but the Deer Act does apply to them so far as legal weapons are concerned.

I am sending you this e-mail to ask for some information on a species of deer called Père David deer. I heard of them many years ago but for the last decade or so I've heard nothing. Indeed, I have never heard of them being stalked, either in Britain or overseas. Can you give me any information on this type of deer?

These interesting, if rather ungainly deer originated in China. They were spotted in 1865 by a missionary, Père David, in the Imperial Hunting Park near Peking. They had been extinct elsewhere, possibly for a thousand years or more. Previously unknown to science, various attempts were made to obtain specimens for western zoos, but breeding was only successful from 1898, and only at Woburn Park in Bedfordshire. Meanwhile the original stock in Peking had been nearly wiped out by escapes following floods and the survivors were killed during the Boxer Rising in 1900. So for years Woburn hosted the sole living representatives of the species.

They are large deer, standing 122 cm at the shoulder, bright chestnut in summer with a blackish stripe down the spine and an unusually long tail. In winter they are iron grey. The stags have peculiar multi-point antlers with a wrong-way-round look to them. A long tine at the back helps in their habit of spooning mud on their backs and of catching up dry grass onto the antlers during the rut until the stag resembles a haystack.

The best place to see Père David deer is at Woburn, but since World War II they have been sold to many parks and zoos. Breeding has not been found as easy as with other deer. Although there have been a few escapes, none have been released in the wild in this country. In 1985 twenty-two deer were sent to China as a gift from the Marquess of Tavistock to the People of China. They were released in part of the old Imperial Hunting Park, so they have at long last returned home.

Is the population of deer in England still increasing?

A lot of people would like to know the full answer to that one! We just don't have the information. What one can say is that several species are steadily increasing their range, and that could well indicate a further growth in numbers.

In general, reds are probably fairly static. Roe may have declined from their peak in the period 1950–70 as the post-war plantations become older and less attractive to them, but they are still spreading into the northern and southern Midland counties, also up the Welsh border and well into the Principality. Cornwall and Kent have also recently been penetrated.

Two problem species are fallow and sika, not only because of their spread, but the large herds congregating on farmland in many parts of the country create real problems. Numbers of both must have swelled in recent years.

Muntjac continue their march north and west from East Anglia and the East Midlands though colonisation appears to be slower when they encounter woodlands already fully occupied by roe. Eventually their northern spread may be limited by climate, especially if we ever get another severe winter. Even the Chinese water deer is reported from new locations in the East Midlands, so drawing a pretty broad brush one could say that we now have more deer than ever country-wide, although in some localities, due to active control or other factors, the pressure may be less.

I have just been in Germany, where they seem to know a lot about telling the age of deer from the tooth wear. Is this an area where we can learn from Europe, or has it all been thoroughly researched already?

Up to the age when the last molar erupts (about ten months in roe, up to thirty months in red and fallow) the age of a deer is easy to estimate. In the following year the cusps are high and sharp before the action of chewing the cud starts to wear them down.

Climatic factors are likely to differ abroad. In the UK the speed of this eroding process varies according to the type and condition of the vegetation the animal eats. Hard food such as heather produces quicker wear than the buds, leaves and young twigs. If the soil is sandy and abrasive a comparatively young animal can have worn teeth giving the impression of one much older. Like people, deer from calcium-rich areas may in any case have stronger teeth to start with.

Age estimation is always fraught with difficulties and anomalies so it is better to look at all the signs, for example the ridges at the angle of the lower jaw which become more pronounced with age, and the central suture (the wiggly centre line of the skull) which becomes more complex. Also the thickness and comparative smoothness of the skull: the condition of the bone over the eye sockets is a good guide. In the case of a male the

As an indicator of age, tooth wear alone can be very misleading. More can be learned from the ridges at the corner of the lower jawbone where the chewing muscles are attached and which become more pronounced with age.

As successive antlers are shed a wedge-shaped piece of bone is lost from each coronet, so that they and the coronets slope progressively outwards as age advances.

pedicles tend to become shorter and more fissured, while in roe the coronets slope progressively outwards in older beasts. Have a careful look at all these signs, not just wear on the teeth – and make your own estimate. There will still be quite a lot of guess-work in it!

One reads in continental sporting books of deer needing salt and that salt blocks would attract them. Do the deer in this country have the same need, as they don't seem very interested in the blocks I have put out!

The need animals have for salt is something of a mystery. I have never found a satisfactory veterinary answer to the benefit they get from it, and I have a feeling that the success the Continentals have is partly due to a habit built up over many years which has left the deer with a taste for it, the young following others by imitation. Maybe also, our Atlantic climate may bring salt-laden air in from the sea, overcoming any possible deficiency. Fallow seem to be quicker to acquire the habit than other species.

A correspondent in Northumberland phoned me recently telling me that his roe do seem attracted to some Salz Paste which he smeared on a stump below an existing deer block. The roe were not touching the paste (which admittedly also contains powerfully aromatic aniseed oil) but were apparently smearing their noses on the exposed wood below the paste and then licking their noses. It's probably worth a trial, and I would be interested to hear the results.

I have a query about tagging and handling deer calves. I am under the impression that calves/fawns should not be handled as the hinds/does would then reject the young animal if she detected human scent. Would hessian sacking mask this?

A great deal is made of this point, to some extent to deter the public from handling, or even worse, trying to 'rescue' young deer which are lying doggo until the mother returns in the mistaken notion that they have been abandoned, or merely because they look pretty.

Any unnecessary disturbance to young wild deer should be avoided. However, for research and other good reasons, tagging is permissible, given trained and sympathetic handling. Informed opinion takes the view that once a calf or fawn has been licked dry soon after birth the mother–young bond is well-enough established to survive the brief human contact involved in ear tagging by skilled personnel. I have no experience of using hessian, but feel that this would add yet another strange odour to the fawn and in addition hamper the operation.

There is a lot of talk about safeguarding the genetic purity of red deer sub-species and that for this reason stock of park origin should not be allowed to be liberated in the Highlands in an effort to improve the size and antlers of the native strain. Can you say whether the Highland reds are in fact a separate sub-species?

About twelve sub-species have been recognised worldwide, although scientific proof of their separate identity is arguable. Scottish red deer have been given sub-specific status as *Cervus elaphus scoticus* and suggestions are made that the pure strain only exists on some Hebridean islands. Only the advance of DNA analysis will prove or disprove this. On the mainland at least, the fact is that since early Victorian times animals have been brought north and liberated on the hill. All too likely this extended to many of the islands as well.

Any long-term effect these releases have had is less than one would imagine. Often a park-bred stag would fail to prosper in the harsh conditions and even if he was successful in mating with a number of hinds for possibly a couple of seasons, genetic dilution would tend to iron out any imported characteristics after a while. The spread of Japanese sika, involving a large and incursive population, is a much more potent threat.

Apart from genetics, efforts over the last century or more to 'improve the breed' of hill deer were limited by the environment itself. Highland reds have adapted to poor browse and savage weather by becoming smaller and hardier than their woodland cousins. Deer and habitat management would have brought much better results than expensive but necessarily small-scale imports of large-antlered specimens, many of which lacked the grace as well as the stamina of the natives.

I am keen to find out a little more about Chinese water deer dentition as it is a gap in my knowledge. One of these has large 'tusks' but recently emerged premolars. Is it a juvenile? Is diet a factor (as in antler growth) or is trophy size purely a genetic lottery? Do the tusks grow throughout life or are they fixed in size once emerged?

I'm no expert on the species, but have noticed that tusk size doesn't necessarily relate to age. In fact many old bucks have broken tusks because of the way they use them. According to my copy of the *Handbook of British Mammals* (Southern) no mammal has teeth that enlarge through life. However, like wild boar, Chinese water deer have tusks which are initially hollow, rather than solid like human teeth, and they do elongate at least into middle age.

So far as I know, no research has been done on the factors influencing tusk size in Chinese water deer but I think it's reasonable to assume that nutrition in youth rather than heredity is the most important factor in their tooth size.

Now that we seem to be having an occasional 'old-fashioned' winter, with a good deal of frost, is there any hope of it having any effect on the muntjac population? Either to reduce numbers or prevent the apparently inexorable spread of this unwelcome alien?

It is still possible we will get a significant fall of snow sooner or later. Reeves' muntjac are not basically well adapted to severe weather, having originated in southeast China. Because they are non-seasonal breeders, a proportion of the young will be born in winter. However, the species appears to have adapted itself to conditions in this country, possibly too well, and they are proving fairly hardy.

The most significant die-off was in the winter of 1963, when in some places it was estimated that 70 per cent of the population died. The limited area of the country colonised by muntjac at that time lay under deep snow for many weeks, added to extreme cold. With our climate changing, the chances of such extreme weather for a long enough period to lead to a heavy die-off appear to be receding. In addition, now that a large part of England is inhabited by muntjac, one could expect recolonisation to balance any local die-off comparatively quickly.

There is another hazard posed by even short periods of fairly deep snow – that is, the difficulty a short-legged animal has in getting about and especially escaping from danger. The fox is a major predator of muntjac and is able to run over crusted snow while hoofed deer flounder. Now that we have wild boar they may take to eating muntjac fawns. Loose dogs, always a concern, can also snap them up, or just by causing them to run away, make them use up vital reserves of energy.

To answer your query, my own feeling is that we have to manage all our deer, and not rely on nature.

I don't know what all the fuss is about the white roe in Scotland. Are they so very rare, because I have two which regularly come into our paddock with some other brown ones? One is pure white, the other creamy-coloured. I haven't been able to see whether they have pink eyes. I'm sure they are roe because they don't have any spots. People say there are one or two others in the woods round here, so is it just a bit of silly-season journalism?

The white deer in Scotland has raised a lot of interest because it is a roe, and is something of a rarity. From what you tell me, the deer coming into your paddock are fallow which do show a variety of colours, white among them. One colour phase of fallow seen in parks, known as *menil* is chestnut with prominent white spots and this does persist even in the winter coat. Common-coloured fallow are brown flecked with white in summer with a white belly. Their backs turn chocolate brown in winter and the spotting is hidden. Then there are black and white varieties, neither of which show spots.

In addition to their larger size, fallow are distinguished from roe by their long and mobile tails. Bucks have palmated (shovel-shaped) antlers. White fawns, as you observed, are more creamy.

Pure white roe may be albino, although not necessarily. From the photo of the Scottish deer its eyes appeared to be normal. Black roe do occur – a black doe was shot in Dorset a few years ago, and they can be seen commonly in North Holland. Parti-coloured roe with normal colour and varying areas of white are reported from time to time. One Dorset doe had a white spot just where a stalker would place his bullet! Surprisingly, she survived a number of years during which the spot grew bigger. If she had lived she might, or might not, have finished up white all over.

4 Antlers

Our fascination with the variety and complexity of deer antlers goes back for a thousand years and more. In the nineteenth century some vast collections were amassed, especially in the German states. Curiously, these were often purchased, rather than proving the skill of the owner. For example Count Arco-Zinneberg had no fewer than four thousand hanging in his palace in Munich for which he was said to have paid sixty thousand pounds – a fortune in the currency of those days. Possibly the most famous acquisition was the Moritzburg sixty-six pointer red stag which was shot in 1696 by the future King of Prussia. His son, keener on his army than on stalking, exchanged this head for a 'Company of tall Grenadiers'. In fact, it is palmated, not very large and something of a monstrosity but enormously prized in those days as a piece of Gothic one-upmanship.

The cycle of rapid growth and annual shedding involves a considerable drain on the animal's resources and to our eyes might seem wasteful. At the same time the influences of heredity, nutrition, and apparently inexplicable variation in size, symmetry and sheer beauty fascinate, inform and intrigue everyone who takes an interest in deer. One might assume that their principal advantage to the bearer would be as weapons of offence and defence, but experiments on caribou in which different sizes of antlers could be clipped in turn on to one beast showed that antler size and status (and therefore breeding success) are strongly linked. Nonetheless, one is a bit sorry for the caribou stag concerned, who must have been a bit confused in the end.

As antler growth is hormone-controlled, any upset to the glands, especially reproductive glands, can cause of all sorts of strange malforma-tions. The most extreme of these is the peruke head which grows uncontrollably but never hardens. Most commonly seen in roe deer, this condition can be produced by deliberate or accidental castration in other species.

Anyone who has visited the Neolithic flint mines at Grimes Graves in Norfolk will have been impressed by the way red deer antlers – hundreds of them – were used as digging tools. They are mostly cast antlers, which the Stone Age children must have been sent out into the woods to find, and in

A mature roebuck's six-point antlers give him an impressive appearance.

preference left-hand antlers which make handier picks for a right-handed digger. I made one myself which was surprisingly effective, but wore down quickly. One wonders how many of our ancient monuments – barrows and tumuli – must have been carved out of the landscape using antler picks.

There is a very ugly roebuck on my ground. He is, however, quite young. Is he likely to have the same sort of malformed antlers all his life, or do they vary from year to year?

A lot of malformations are caused by damage to the growing velvet and will not persist. Where the bone of the pedicle is damaged (or there is some bodily injury) then the malformation is likely to persist. Some bucks in captivity, where the cast antlers were kept each year, have grown really ugly heads at some stage, only to produce splendid typical ones afterwards. In the wild, of course, a buck growing dissimilar antlers in successive years would not be recognised as the same individual.

If you have a big cull of young bucks, then it's probably best to weed out ugly heads especially if the owner looks at all poor in condition.

Do you ever find muntjac with more than four points? I thought I saw one in Oxfordshire when I was stalking last spring, but it didn't stand still long enough to see – or to shoot it, for that matter.

Muntjac are not like roe in the variety of their antlers, even the largest only having four points. However, just recently one or two multi-pointers have come in for CIC measuring. I saw a magnificent six-pointer from Norfolk at the St Hubert Club trophy show one year, so it can happen! In all deer, antler growth is affected by the level of nutrition while they are growing, so as muntjac become established in our lush woodlands this type of luxuriant growth in the form of extra points is not unlikely.

In late March/early April I shot a fallow pricket which was in soft velvet. I have been stalking for about six years and this is the first time I have come across this at this time of year. Can you tell me if it is common?

Normally fallow deer shed their antlers in May, shedding the velvet just before the rut, in late August or early September. Yearling bucks are different. Donald and Norma Chapman, in their classic book *Fallow Deer*, when describing antler growth in the buck's first year state that the pedicles are well developed in March at the age of nine months and that in precocious animals the antler itself may be well developed at this time of year. The pedicles continue to grow during the spring and by May/June, when the fawns are almost a year old, the antlers are well grown, fraying in August. Judging by the photograph, your buck's longer antler might be four to six inches long. It is difficult to be sure about the age, but it is certainly young.

To see a pricket so well forward in March is unusual, but fallow are less reliable in their patterns of antler growth than some other species. For example, the younger fallow bucks in Richmond Park, to quote the same book, are the last to clean in autumn, while the twelfth Duke of Bedford said that in Woburn it is the oldest and biggest which are the last. In my experience of other parks the latter case is more normal. There is always something new to observe with deer!

All summer I have had a yearling roebuck on my ground which stays in velvet. Even at the end of the rut he was still in dark velvet, showing no sign of it drying. He has an ear-high four-point head and is in every way but this in excellent condition. What is the matter with him? Is it possible that he is a potential peruke, and if so how long will it take to develop?

The fact this young buck is apparently in good health does seem to indicate that some hormonal imbalance, rather than disease or injury, has prevented the normal drying and fraying process. Unless this corrects itself quite soon, the growth of a peruke is likely at some stage.

How rapidly a peruke can grow has only been documented, surprisingly, on an elderly doe. This tame animal grew short antlers in velvet, as some old does do, and only after a couple of years did this suddenly enlarge into a real peruke. In the case of a male, I guess the process might be much quicker, but the change from remaining in velvet to producing exaggerated growth might involve something of a threshold. The natural surge of antler growth which occurs in late winter is the likeliest time, but it would be very interesting if a watch could be kept up on this interesting animal and his progress monitored. If he has developed into a peruke by next summer, it would be a kindness to shoot him because in hot weather the antler tissue gets infected and possibly fly-blown, leading to a painful death.

I have just shot a strange roe. It has massive antlers in velvet which look diseased. When I gralloched it, I couldn't see much in the way of testicles, and though it appeared to be male, it had teats. I suppose this is what is called a peruke, but could it be half-male and half-female? Someone said it is an 'antlered doe' but it has no female externals except for the teats. Was it right to shoot it?

I have had a careful look at your photos, and the animal is definitely a buck, though the testes are rudimentary. Male hormones produced by the testes do not make antlers grow, but they control the hardening process in a normal animal. So if the supply of male hormones fails, either by injury, birth defect or disease, then antler growth continues uncontrolled, leading to the formation of a mass of antler tissue in velvet as you have seen. This is known as a peruke (or perruque) because it looks like a wig. Sometimes the mass of antler grows down over the eyes, blinding the buck. Eventually the peruke becomes infected and the beast dies.

Antlered does are found regularly. They are usually very old females which (as in some other species) have started to show male characteristics. Normally the antlers are short, but cases have been known where this, too, has formed a peruke. The antlers are always in velvet.

The half-way stage – a hermaphrodite – commonly has the externals of a female but grows antlers which are clean and hard due to the presence of some quantity of male hormone. Such animals are really rare, but the

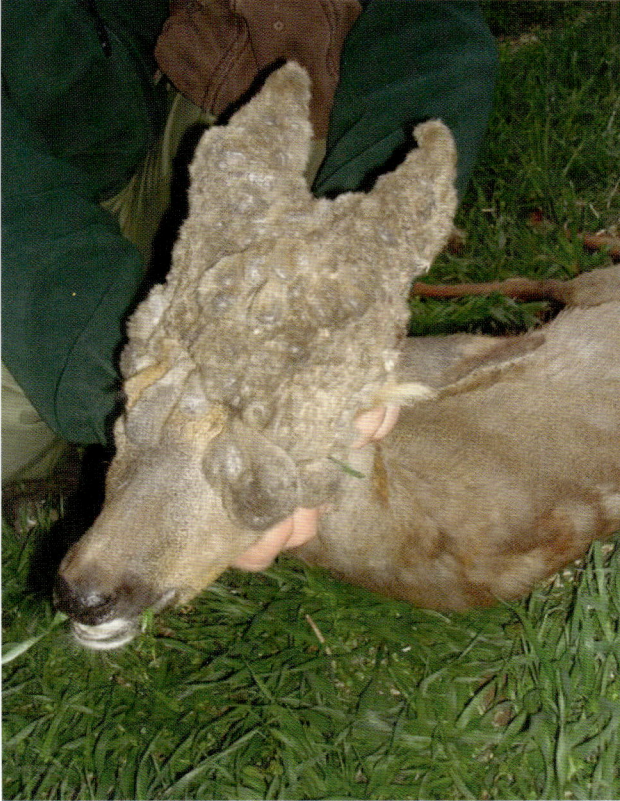

A fully developed peruke head. It is likely this buck would have died quite soon as the soft tissue became fly-blown and infected.

condition for some reason is more often found in roe than in other deer breeds.

A few peruke bucks turn up most years, I suspect that the majority have damaged their testicles through jumping barbed wire. If you see one, there is no point in sparing it, as the expectation of life in that condition is pretty short.

Our postman picked up a deer antler the other day and he wonders what animal grew such a massive thing, and are there many here in Norfolk?

What he found is the cast antler of a mature red stag. It has 'all its rights' (brow, bay and tray tines) and three for the crown. If both antlers were the same it would have been a royal.

At a guess it is probably a beast past his best. As one can see, the lower tines are longer than the tops so that the tips make a triangle. In younger stags the top points or crown tend to be longer, so that the tips make a rectangle. In the jargon, he may be starting to 'go back'.

Red deer are well established in Norfolk. Some of their ancestors were 'outliers' or deer that had escaped after release for hunting by the Norwich Staghounds. This was a pack hunting the Carted Stag; that is to say semi-domesticated deer were released on the day of the hunt and were normally brought to bay without harm by the hounds before being returned to their park next to the kennels in a cart, hence the name.

Casting and re-growing antlers each year is a considerable strain on the resources of a deer. Rich feeding in the fields allows some of the Norfolk red deer to grow unusually long antlers.

I have been given a roe skull with fantastic pearling right up to the tops, but it is very light in weight and the bone seems very brittle, even porous. One stalking friend has said it is a 'mossed head' and the other a 'peruke'. What does this all mean, and what is the cause?

A typical mossed head with exaggerated pearling on antlers which are fully hardened, though usually porous.

Roe, more than other deer species, are liable to grow malformed antlers. One cause of this is temporary or permanent malfunction of the hormone supply, primarily testosterone. Rather surprisingly in a way, antler growth takes place normally when the hormone supply is at a low ebb. When the reproductive cycle kicks in, rising levels of hormone stop growth and cause the antler to harden and the velvet covering to decay and fall off. Any malfunction of the hormone supply, when the antlers are in velvet or otherwise, can create abnormal growth. Castration has the most immediate effect. The antlers of a buck in velvet at the time of castration continue to grow in an uncontrolled way, producing a wig-like mass, which gives rise to the name peruke (or perruque). If the velvet on a peruke is stripped away, the antler mass will be found to be soft and porous, as you describe.

If the interruption to the hormone supply is only temporary, the antler mass will harden with a resumption of supply, resulting in unnaturally heavy pearling which has hardened. Even then, it is liable to be lighter in density and may be fragile.

So, as you have found, the dividing lines between normal antler, mossed head and peruke are matters of opinion, even between experts!

Do roebucks in velvet feel the cold? During the recent bitter weather I saw plenty of young bucks and does, but the seniors who are more forward with their antler growth don't appear. Can they get frostbite?

The antlers of any male deer while they are growing feel warm to the touch due to the abundant blood supply in the velvet. I think they might well add to a buck's discomfort in strong cold winds and make him seek shelter more than the well-insulated does. Younger bucks are showing less antler growth in January and February and might be less affected.

Yes, growing antlers can get frostbitten so that when they eventually harden the tips will be missing. This is a well-known phenomenon in Central Europe, but is less common in Britain because of our milder climate.

There may be another reason for your seeing more does in late winter – the foetus which has been semi-dormant since the rut last August attaches itself by a placenta and commences rapid growth. The doe is likely to react by feeding more intensively.

In the spring, older deer start to shed their coats earlier than the youngsters. They can look extremely bedraggled and ragged. The winter hair loses its insulating quality even before it falls out, and if this coincides with a period of cold wet weather, they certainly do suffer miserably. A heavy infestation of lice, often associated with poor condition, exaggerates the problem and one can see the unfortunate animals literally shivering in the cold wet weather we often seem to have in April.

We have noticed that the roe we are seeing on most of my ground are all in hard horn and have been for a while now, is that from high up on Dartmoor to low ground around here?

Yet on an estate up the Teign valley most of the deer we have seen, are still in velvet. Now again we come back to a question of genetics or is it location? The food should be as good as in other places.

One thing I have thought of is that everything else has access to bordering fields, but these deer live in a large mixed deciduous woodland with a lot of rhododendron. What if anything do you think would cause the difference?

One can only speculate on this one. The general rule is that older bucks tend to fray earlier than the younger ones. Then if the weather turns cold and dry just when the velvet is due to come off, the bucks feel less like fraying and the velvet hardens and is subsequently difficult to detach, especially with well-pearled antlers.

If the Teign valley deer were still in full soft velvet while yours were clean, then there is a distinct difference of fraying date in comparison, but if the velvet is mostly hard in the old bucks, maybe the upper Teign valley has a slightly distinct climate, enough to inhibit fraying temporarily, though nobody could claim that Dartmoor is particularly mild!

The other possibility is that the deciduous wet acid woodland with rhododendron clumps typical of the skirts of Dartmoor provides fairly poor browse and the roe in this sort of habitat are in poorer condition than those with access to the fields.

I have read somewhere that if a deer is injured, say a broken leg or something like that, he will grow a malformed antler the following year, but the malformation will be on the opposite side to the injury.

A buck I shot the other day had, I think, been hit by a car, anyway he had a mended foreleg and some ribs cracked. When I saw him he was limping a bit. He had a normal six-point head, one antler had a slight outward curl, but that was on the injured side. Is this very unusual?

It's no good writing rules for deer – they don't read the books! This is something about which it is extremely difficult to be dogmatic. You shoot a buck with an old injury and he has some malformation on the opposite side; if you are one of those chaps who like to theorise, you say 'that proves the point'. Another time the malformation is on the same side, so 'that's the exception which proves the rule' and so on.

I have seen a lot of heads which conformed to the 'opposite side' rule, but equally a considerable number that did not. It could be argued that if a buck has a posture like the Leaning Tower of Pisa due to an injury, his antlers when they are growing might attempt to grow towards the vertical, thus giving them a list to port (or starboard) which would be very obvious when he is shot. One knows, too, that there is a degree of crossing over in an animal's physical make-up which lends weight to the theory.

Of course injury is not the only cause of malformation. There is a widespread notion that antler shape is inherited and the red stags with multi-point, almost palmated antlers which trace their ancestry back to Warnham stock bear this out. A buck with malformed antlers not caused by accident might pass this tendency on to his offspring.

Some recent research in Slovenia has suggested atmospheric pollution and the stress resulting from it as additional causes of misshapen antlers. Rapid annual growth picks up variations in the habitat year by year and the researchers found a close correlation with a local decline in lead pollution in a series of roe antlers shot between 1925 and 2004. A further series of antlers, from another district, of bucks shot between 1960 and 2002 showed greater asymmetry where lead pollution was greatest. Our roe may be subject to different types of stress, but such factors as human disturbance could also be the cause of slight or major lack of symmetry in our deer.

My personal feeling about the 'opposite side' theory is that the case is not proven – but it is fun trying!

Why are so many of our roebucks late in shedding their velvet this year? Normally we expect more bucks to be free of velvet by early April, but this year it was difficult to find one decent buck then which was completely clean. Since that time a lot of bucks still have velvet attached although it has dried and looks like leather.

Young bucks and those without very heavy pearling can fray very quickly, leaving the new antler either completely white or bloodstained. If the buck gets it right, practically the whole sheath of velvet can peel away like a glove, while others with large pearls and very prominent coronets have to work at it because of the complexity of their antlers.

My feeling is that rapid velvet fraying needs a spell of mild weather, either because it encourages the buck to fray actively or because the velvet itself is limp and easily detached in open weather. If it turns cold or very dry just at the critical time, velvet becomes hard, just as you describe. Young bucks, to whom fraying is part of the necessary business of competition, soon get their antlers clean though it may take longer in dry than in damp springs. In contrast the major bucks get on with life without bothering to fray excessively, as is their nature. Territory determination is mostly settled with barking and other threats because of their formidable appearance and the remnants of dry velvet, especially at the back of each antler, can remain there, held in place by the pearling. I see the result of this so often in trophies brought in for measurement. They have a white stripe up the back where remaining velvet has been stripped off after boiling out.

In early September I shot a roebuck in full, dry velvet. Just in the condition one would expect to see them in March normally. It was fat and was fully equipped with male attributes. Was it ill, or what? Can you explain, or do you need to see the head?

That really is a curious one. The fact that it had testicles and a typical head in dry velvet seems to indicate no hormonal upset. The only theory I can suggest is that it was a case of two sets of antlers being grown in a single year, the first being shed about late May. The phenomenon has been known in Père David deer and we do know of two authenticated cases in roe, one in Scotland and one in Germany, both inevitably of bucks in captivity and with a high level of nutrition. The odds of a similar case in the wild in good habitat are quite good, but proving it is another thing. I would expect the head and antlers to show nothing out of the ordinary. Sika deer subjected to artificial 'nights', the equivalent of being flown to the Antipodes, have been induced to grow two sets of antlers, but that is different.

Visiting the New Forest last year I saw the antlers of a pair of roe which had become locked together. This must be a very unusual occurrence considering the simple shape of roe antlers. Do you know of any other cases, or is this pair unique?

Of course this is much more rare in roe than among deer species with more complicated antlers, such as fallow or caribou. I have heard of nine cases in

Interlocked antlers.

Two bucks which locked antlers while fighting and could not disengage.

a stretch of thirty years. Several entanglements were reported in the early 1970s. One pair was found in Northumberland by Mr A Lyell. In this case one of the combatants had a very unusual thirteen-point head which no doubt contributed to the tragedy. His age was estimated at seven years. His opponent was a four-year beast with a fine head of 25.4 cm.

In the south, a pair of interlocked skulls, both standard six-pointers, was picked up by the Late Major-General Lipscombe, who offered his young daughter sixpence (old money) if she could separate them. Luckily she failed! They probably became fixed at the moment when, as happens in all roebuck fights, the two bucks lower their heads and jump together in the same way that rams fight. Presumably the combined force of their impact and an unlucky angle was enough to make the antlers spring slightly and then lock together so that one buck broke his neck and the other miserably starved to death.

Shortly afterwards three other sets were discovered. One pair came from the New Forest, where it was discovered in a recently decomposed state by the New Forest Buckhounds. I expect this is the pair you were shown. Another pair of large, heavily antlered animals was found in Sussex, and a fourth example came from Wiltshire. In this case the contestants were very ill-matched.

Soon after, another tragedy came to light on a farm in Wiltshire. When these animals were found they had been dead some weeks, but during the past rut they had obviously been fencing with one another in a thickly bushed hedgerow, with a maple stem acting as a barrier between. Not only had they locked antlers, but the maple also became involved and they had no chance of freeing themselves. They had clearly been there many days before they died. This again was a well-matched pair of bucks, both with well-developed antlers, one with six points, the other with five.

Like most wild animals roebuck avoid conflict if an alternative is open to them. In the case of two bucks competing for territory, if one is markedly older or stronger than the other, mere barking will probably be sufficient to drive the smaller one away. Fighting is usually a last resort when various demonstrations have failed.

One of my roebucks cast his antlers in the middle of September this year. I think it is a natural cast, rather than an accident, as he seems otherwise perfectly fit. Is this very unusual? He looks fully mature, but not specially old.

If this was entirely natural, it's certainly exceptionally early. Antler cast normally does not start until October. As a rule the older bucks are the first to cast, yearlings being the last towards the end of the year. However, there are exceptions, and this could just be one of these. I have one record of a New Forest buck which had cast on 3 September. Other possibilities are accident, disease or injury. Bucks hit by cars often have their antlers broken off, especially if they were near to casting and therefore the antlers were weakened between pedicle and coronet. The other cause of premature casting is the loss of male hormone, either through internal disease or physical castration, which can happen through getting hung up on a wire fence. As soon as the level of testosterone drops, the antlers will shed and if the supply is not resumed, a peruke head will start to grow until the unfortunate buck has a wig-like growth of antler in velvet on his head (explaining the name). This never cleans, and usually goes putrid, eventually killing the wearer.

I saw a yearling roe buck last month (January) in hard horn. Is there something wrong with him, or is it just unusually late?

As it was a young beast, it is likely to have been healthy but this is unusually late for antler-cast. Normally the old bucks cast towards the end of October with the younger ones following until virtually all are bare-headed or in early velvet by Christmas. In recent years there seems to be a tendency for bucks to show clean antlers much earlier in the year for whatever reason; reports of clean and coloured heads in February are not uncommon. This would suggest that the casting date is also earlier, so that makes this report all the more interesting.

Roe kids at about six months may grow small antlers known as fawn buttons which clean in January and cast in February before the growth of the first true head, but these are unlikely to exceed three to four centimetres in length, and an experienced stalker is most unlikely to be deceived. One in my possession is 4.3 cm long with rudimentary pearling. The finest specimen, a miniscule three-pointer, belonged to a friend in Cumbria who dropped his stalking stick and picked up the stick and cast antler together. By memory it was about thirty millimetres long.

Deer-watching in the New Forest recently, I spotted a sika stag which had either nine or ten points – certainly more than the normal eight. Could it have been a hybrid, or a different sub-species, or do Japanese sika sometimes have multi-point heads?

You raise an interesting point about multi-point sika. The principal source of multi-pointers over the last forty years has indeed been the southern New Forest where sika, thought to be from Powerscourt, escaped from Beaulieu Estate in 1904, to be followed by a release in 1905. Few have been reported in recent years. It has always been assumed that they were pure Japanese, though red deer do now occur in the same area and so hybridism is possible. The presence of another sub-species is very unlikely. What multi-point heads I have seen from the Forest were very typically sika, with upright brows and short points. Definite hybrids, from Wicklow for example, have much more of the red deer look about them, although the white tuft on the hock which is so typical of sika seems usually to be retained. Other points to look for are a pale chevron on the forehead and the longer tail.

There was a fairly authoritative paper in the spring 2007 issue of the BDS magazine, 'Sika deer in the New Forest and the Isle of Purbeck', which took the line that both communities were reasonably pure Japanese sika from the Nagasaki area of Japan.

This buck was shot as a cull, but seems to have several potential coronets scattered about some very heavy pearling, with two plain spikes above. It was not old and was in good condition. Can you explain what has happened?

Puzzling over the cause of antler malformations is always interesting, but has to be guesswork to a degree.

Examining this head, both upper spikes are normal, possibly what one would expect on a good yearling, and rise from rudimentary coronets above the area of heavy pearling.

Everything below this is abnormal, including the small spikes which look like attempts at complete antlers.

A curious malformation, possibly showing the previous year's yearling unshed antlers surrounded by additional bone in the next season.

My construction of events is that the top spikes are actual yearling antlers, but at the time when they were due to cast the buck suffered some temporary upset to his hormonal system through disease or injury. When he recovered, one would have expected new antler growth to surround the old, as I have seen, notably in the crop of 'knob stags' which afflicted the red deer of Thetford many years ago. In these stags one could see the division as a faint line between last year's spikes and the knobbly growth round it, like holding something in your fist. They always appeared to be in good health but the one I shot had very small testicles.

The same phenomenon can occasionally be observed in fallow.

I know that some roebucks in their first year grow small antlers which fall off in early spring before the growth of the first true head. Does this occur in other species?

There is no mention in the literature, either for red or fallow deer of this phenomenon, probably due to the different antler cycle in the larger species. It would be interesting to hear from any readers who have seen anything of the sort.

There is, however, some information about this from the Czech Republic. Dr Karel Klusac reported that in 1978 and 1983, years which were notable for an extremely high acorn crop and a mild winter, some of the well-developed male fallow fawns in two parks were seen to grow small antlers. These grew through December, were clean of velvet by March and were shed as small knobs in April before the normal first head was grown. In his opinion this was the result of high feeding and kinder weather conditions than usual.

It is surprising that even in the extravagant days of the late 1800s, when landowners vied with one another to produce the finest heads in their park deer, nobody recorded the growth of buttons in their fawns. There is no mention of it in Walter Winans' *Deer Breeding for Fine Heads*, nor in either JG Millais' *British Deer and their Horns*, or his monumental *The Mammals of Great Britain and Ireland*, although he was much more of a naturalist than deadly shot and showman Winans. GK Whitehead in *The Encyclopedia of Deer* only mentions them as occurring in roe deer. I find it difficult to believe that this is the case and can only think it must have shown up in one park or another and was overlooked.

I live in a small village in Devon. I've been stalking for many years with my brother or on my own and during this time neither of us have ever come across a roebuck with a head like this. The crown has grown so big that it has joined from the base to about four inches up; it's a magnificent head, and the animal weighed as much as a fallow pricket. After showing this head to a gamekeeper and a life-long stalker they recommended I sent a picture in to the Shooting Times & Country Magazine *as they had never seen one like it before either – have you?*

This very interesting trophy is what is known as a coalesced head and something of a rarity. It is a very old buck and in its youth probably had pedicles which were fairly close together. Through time and successive antler-shedding, the pedicles become progressively thicker and shorter. In this case contact between the pedicles has become so intimate that when these antlers were growing, they did so as one up to the point where they bifurcate. Such antlers are shed as one although at an earlier stage the union is not complete and the cast antlers may be separated.

Two examples of this malformation are pictured in my book *The Roe Deer – Conservation of a Native Species*, (page 106). The first example I encountered was on a farm rubbish dump, and I bought it for sixpence (2½p)! Most stalkers these days, however, would, like you, recognise it as a trophy to be treasured.

As you can see from the photos I shot this deer as a cull buck back at the start of May, but I fear I may have made a orphan of a kid. Is this common in roe does? Is it hormone related or environmental? Can we take steps to stop this in other does?

Lastly have you any tips on how to not make the mistake again, as the deer had no visible anal tuft of hair at a distance!

I understand your distress at this completely unavoidable mistake. I'm afraid that she was in milk and therefore it would be worth looking for the fawn to put it out of misery.

An antlered doe. If the antlers remain in velvet it is female. If they harden and clean, the animal may be hermaphrodite.

Growing antlers, usually very much of this sort, is not uncommon in roe. The most extreme case was a tame fawn owned by the late Kenneth Macarthur, who produced successive sets of twins for years; she then grew antlers which eventually turned into a full peruke. A post mortem showed the presence of a small quantity of testicular cells in the vicinity of the ovary. Most antlered does are pretty old. Growing some male characteristics signals a change in hormone balance in the body, although not sufficient at the stage of your doe to inhibit breeding. The same phenomenon can be seen in other species, including our own.

On a practical level, a doe in summer coat does not display much of an anal tuft. In addition, roe in the south of England normally have a lemon yellow or even brownish target, while north-country targets are whiter. This makes identifying an antlered doe even more difficult. I have made the same mistake, as have many other stalkers, and no matter how sad one is at the event, if it looks exactly like a poor yearling, there is not much one can do unless she is in sight for long enough to observe urination.

In the last week of February I saw a roebuck which had just finished fraying his new antlers. Isn't this exceptionally early?

Certainly it is early, but these days not exceptionally so. Half a century ago one expected some bucks in the southwest of England to be clean in March: the farther west, the earlier by a few days. In Dorset in the 1960s when I was out every day, my dates for the first buck to clean were regularly from 1–4 April, with the majority of adults clean by mid-April. Only in 1966 was a buck seen with clean antlers on 15 March, with the majority following by early April. West Dorset admittedly was a bit earlier.

Lately the season has advanced steadily into March. Whether this is due to global warming or to other factors is hard to guess. April is now an important time in the roe stalking year. The old idea of starting the buck season on 1 May has long gone. Very soon after this the cover has thickened enough to make stalking in woodland very difficult. As recently as 2009 three bucks were reported to be clean before the end of February, two in Northumberland (14 and 17 February), the other in Dorset (20 February).

Considering the resources drained by male deer in growing antlers annually, wouldn't it be more energy efficient if they only replaced them, say, every two or three years? After all, there isn't too much difference in size, complexity or appearance between the antlers grown, for example, by red stags of two and three years of age. If it's a bad year, the next head may even be smaller, especially in the case of roe. Is there some mechanism which restricts them to an annual cycle, or is there so much advantage that survival of the fittest is involved?

Certainly discarding two large bones yearly does involve the sacrifice of minerals, protein and other valuable and often scarce resources, which more or less goes to prove that there are major advantages in the possession of antlers. Experiments with caribou have shown that replacing a large set of antlers with a smaller set has an immediate effect on the social status of the individual, and thus on his likely ability to mate and pass on his genes. A cock pheasant losing his tail feathers suffers in the same way, so this has to do with appearance, not with the utility of antlers as weapons of offence or defence. Long spikes with no points would probably serve better in that respect.

Basically the antler cycle is determined by the influence of daylight on various glands and is therefore essentially annual. Biologically it would be difficult to envisage, as it were, a 'Green' or energy-efficient two- or three-year replacement cycle.

5 Stalking

P ossibly for the sake of political correctness, we tend to talk about 'culling' or 'management' when in fact we mean the intensely challenging and at times thrilling sport of deer stalking. My old friend, the artist Frank Wallace, had no such reservations. He had pursued big game everywhere but still dearly loved his roe stalking. In his book *Hunting Winds* he wrote of a long, hot, brambly and exhausting stalk in the rut which was nearly foiled at the last minute by the sudden appearance of a doe 'Hot and miserable, I glared at her blurred image' (he wore spectacles). Luckily all was well and he got the buck, the best he ever shot, but doesn't one know those heart-stopping moments!

Recently I had a marvellous letter from Charlie Enderle in Aberdeen-shire whose description of the long-drawn tensions and uncertainties of woodland stalking deserve to be shared.

It was just after a cold snap while out scouting for the forthcoming doe season. I left the house early well before daylight and was in the wood in plenty of time but I could not finding anything – no sign, no tracks, nothing. After several uneventful hours I had all but given up and was heading for home. For some reason I decided to have a quick glass over a dry stone dike into the neighbouring field. I did not have permission to enter the adjacent ground but I decided to have a look anyway in case some were out feeding, and there was a doe not forty yards full broad side to me. So I sat down and watched her for some time, trying to find out more about her and where she would go. Would she come on to my ground or not? Then ten yards in front of her I glimpsed the tips of an antler and that was it: the heart started to pump and the harder I looked the harder and faster my heart pumped. The doe walked at ninety degrees to me and ended up beside him blocking my view. Then she disappeared behind a gorse bush and he had vanished. I had not got a good look at him yet but I knew he was either the main buck or the satellite as I had been trying all summer to get either one.

My head was starting to pound with the rhythm of my heart. Had I lost him? With the end of the season so close it was today or never, so I stayed still and waited keeping my glasses stuck to the spot where I last seen the doe, then, further up the hedgerow I caught a glimpse of white. There they were! I knew that there was a old trail up ahead that leads into the wood that I was in. They were coming on to my ground about one hundred yards up ahead of where I was.

Time to move, and move fast if there was to be any chance of a shot as once in the wood there was twenty yards of fallen mature pine, then a clearing of forty yards and after that what can only be described as a mixture of impenetrable plantation and more fallen pines. If they made it across the clearing that was it; I would not see him again until next year. So I jumped down from the dike, running back into the wood some fifty yards to give me the best possible angle along the clearing, still keeping my eye on the old trail, hoping that I would be right. But before I could get there I heard a crash and the sound of breaking branches (it sounded more like a moose than a roe). I turned and there he was, pushing his way through the fallen pines. His head came up under a big old pine trunk; the gap must have been just the right size as it looked more like a bolt hole for a rabbit than for a roe.

As he came up from under the trunk it was then that I got a good look at him and my heart stopped; I could not believe the sight in front of me. At that we both locked eyes and then he took off with such speed and effortless grace. It was almost magical, he stopped right on the edge of the clearance as quick as he had started, and looked back at me giving me the perfect shoulder shot at about eighty yards. Before I had a second look I heard my rifle go off and the buck stumbled and ran into the remaining standing mature pine.

I had taken the shot as if by instinct. Now to rush after him or wait? It was all I could do to control myself. I knew the shot was good but I forced myself to sit. I laid out my shooting sticks, one pointing to where I had taken the shot and the other to where I had last seen him twenty yards to the left of the shot. It was an eternity. After ten minutes I went to the shot site but after four or five minutes I could not find a blood trail, nothing.

'Take it easy,' I said to myself, 'you know the shot was good – keep looking'. Then I saw it, how could I miss it! A good blood trail (like the yellow brick road in the Wizard of Oz but red). 'Wait some more,' I thought, 'the last thing you want now is to scare him off. Just in case sit back down for another five minutes, if nothing else to recover yourself.'

Five more minutes; I started off on the trail. It was not hard to do – every blade of grass, every tree had a six inch red flash across it: the harder I looked the more of a trail I could see. Then around one last trunk not even twenty-five yards from the shot site there he was, and that's when I realised just how big a buck he was. Not just his antlers but his whole body. Shortly after, during the long haul out of the wood back to the truck I really knew how big he was, as it was nearly quarter of a mile, all in some of the finest Scottish Highland scenery.

The best bit of it occurred in December when I was out stalking does, in the same wood not fifty yards from where the buck fell. The snow came on and was almost a white-out when out of the blue, or should I say white, came this monster buck maybe twenty yards from me. He still had both antlers and makes the one I got look like the bronze I sent to you three years ago. I am not sure which was the higher ranking and which the satellite, but I will be keeping a close eye on this one and with any luck I will bump into him this summer!

Isn't it funny how often, when a big buck has been shot, that another is seen, even bigger than the first? Perhaps that's what keeps us keen and eager. It isn't only the grass which is greener on the other side of the hill! That, to my mind, is what stalking is all about.

For some time I have been interested in deer stalking but have never had the opportunity to go.

I was wondering whether there was anywhere in England (or the UK) where I could be taken by a guide to be shown how to hunt, skin and harvest a deer myself, as well as take some meat home? I do not have a gun licence, but have had limited experience with rifles before.

Should I be allowed to do this, what sort of cost can I expect? I am not keen on trophies, but more keen on filling my fridge and having a fun day or two out!

I would suggest that there are two possible approaches to your needs. If you feel you would like a taste of the sport (and possibly fill the freezer at the same time) then I would suggest you answer a few advertisements for stalking. Tell them what you would like to do and that you do not yet possess a rifle. You can stalk using a borrowed rifle provided the owner accompanies you. This means one-to-one supervision but as you don't want a trophy and would be happy with a yearling buck or a cull doe during the winter, the costs ought to be much less than the red-carpet stuff and should be much easier for a professional stalker to slot in. Ask for some references from previous clients, as not every advertiser can produce what he promises. Prices vary from place to place. The National Gamekeepers' Organisation www.nationalgamekeepers.org.uk can give you details of their stalker members.

You could expect to have some trial shots on a target and enjoy two or three dusk or dawn outings within a weekend. You would need unobtrusive, water proof clothes, comfortable rubber-soled footgear and a pair of binoculars, and be sure to turn up at the given place on time. Some stalkers offer accommodation, which is a bonus.

If stalking really starts to grab you, then the British Deer Society (www.bds.org.uk) and BASC (www.basc.org.uk) run stalkers' courses up and down the country which provide the best possible start to getting the most out of an absorbing hobby. In either event you would probably benefit from studying a basic manual, such as *The Deer Stalking Handbook* by Graham Downing, or my own *Roe Deer – Stalking and Management*, both published by Quiller Press.

What is the best weather to go out woodland stalking?

For most of us – it's when you get the chance! Joking apart, some weather is unpleasant and some downright dangerous, so you do well to ask. Fog is the very worst; not only are deer dimly seen, if at all, but you can't be sure of your background for safety. When in doubt – don't!

High wind makes deer nervous and skittish because they can no longer rely on their noses. Rain and cold wind together makes them miserable. Look in sheltered places, under hedges, in the lee of bale stacks, anywhere, in fact, where conditions are a little less desolate. Having said that, a sudden rainstorm can produce plenty of movement for a period as the deer shift to better cover.

Freshly fallen snow has a disturbing effect on deer. Your best chance is to look under dense conifer stands where the snow is thinner and deer may be attracted by fallen needles or broken-off branches of good browse. Heavy snow can bring down ivy-covered hedgerow trees which will be very attractive. After a day or two there may be more movement, but if the snow is crusted, walking about is like treading on cornflakes and it's better to go to a high seat overlooking any place which catches the early sun. After a cold night the deer may be slow to move, but when the sun rises they like to run about to get warm.

We all visualise lovely summer mornings full of birdsong, and lovely they are. Roe will probably be about fairly early but may lie down a couple of hours after dawn only to move again if the flies get bad – just when you are thinking of breakfast.

Curiously, a warm drizzle can be really good, and deer seem deliberate in their movements and take less notice of a shot.

I only get short weekends for my roe stalking, so every moment is precious. Is it worth going out again after breakfast on the off-chance something is moving?

84

Over-enthusiasm leads too often to over-stalking. Certainly you will find quite a bit of movement during the day, especially if your woods are quiet and not infested with walkers and so on. Actually, if you stalk the same ground much, the deer tend to realise that you are about from first light and round sunset. They can alter their feeding timetable to suit, which is the reason why farm workers often tell you they see more deer than you do!

However, there is a reverse to this coin: if you have only a restricted amount of ground and stalk it every weekend from dawn to dusk you will quickly make the deer shy and nocturnal. One of my clients used to show his keenness by telling of the number of miles he had walked through the wood, and how surprised he was to see fewer and fewer each day. Had they been poached?

If the size of your stalking ground permits, stalk one bit before breakfast, but somewhere else later on. Alternatively, choose a comfortable vantage point and wait there in case something turns up. If you do that, the betting is that your client will soon be asleep and dead to the world until lunch-time!

Do you think that roe in a wild situation, in contrast to semi-tame or hand-reared animals, recognise us as individuals or just as a human animal? What set me wondering was the sight of a roe doe watching me about my work on the game farm last summer. Many times she would stand about 150 metres away up on a hill watching me. As long as I stayed in sight she would watch; if I went into the shed she would then move on. So am I just a curiosity to be watched or am I known by smell or sight or both, or just because I am always there? I assume we must all smell different from each other to animals, otherwise gundogs would have trouble finding their similarly dressed owners on a shoot day.

Deer certainly seem to know the difference between a stalker and someone who wishes them no harm, but how?

To reply to this I think one has to try and look at it from the viewpoint of a deer. Having seen an intruder the first thing they do is to interpret body language. I have often noticed with BDS visits to parks that the deer take little notice of a group of people walking about, but as soon as an over-keen photographer moves or stoops to improve the angle for their shot, this is instantly picked up as a hostile move and the herd takes off. All regular woodland users, stalkers, foresters, keepers or farm workers give their scent to the deer and I have no doubt at all that they come to associate not only the scent but the body language of each passer-by, aggressive or otherwise, and act accordingly. Beyond this, the clothes you wear, probably more by shape and tone than colour, are part of an identification package.

Visiting estates, it is all too clear where a lazy stalker has been shooting from his vehicle because the deer, hearing that engine note, take fright, although they often take little notice of tractors, or even of the farm Land Rover. They are not fools!

I really am confused about the best times to go out roe stalking. Up here in the North, at midsummer it is hardly worth going to bed at all if one is out until dark and out again at first light. Then after a few days I'm too tired to get up at all!

It's no good getting so whacked that you either go to sleep in high seats or just blunder about not enjoying it. Added to that is the real risk of driving a car in the early hours when sleep can hit you without warning.

Of course there are occasions when you are after a particular buck and know his routine that an ambush at first or last light is the only solution. However, looking over my stalking diaries the tradition of first and last light as the most likely times does not have much foundation. Where the summer nights are so short, the deer have to be about in daylight, and the stalker has to get some sleep – sometime, which is more than the midges do.

There are still some general rules that apply. On cold mornings the deer are likely to wait until the sun is up, and then relax on warm banks and in sunny corners. If there are many pigeons about, it is better to let them leave, so that you can move about the woods without a constant clatter.

In the evening there is usually more movement towards dusk, but when a buck looks shadowy, it's better to leave him. Even though he is fairly clear in the scope, the muzzle flash will blind you and leave you with a beast which is difficult to locate. The most successful stalkers in my experience are those who, though keen, take a relaxed attitude to their sport.

During the last doe season I took what I thought was a careful shot with my .270 at a fallow. She humped and staggered off about fifty yards into some woodland. When I followed up there were only a few blood drops and when I put her up in some bushes, she went off again and I didn't find her. What ought I to have done?

It's a miserable business when you lose a beast, and you are right to question what you did. Of course it's easy to say 'take more trouble with your shooting in the first place' but we have all done it. Second, was your rifle properly zeroed?

When a deer 'humps' like that, it is usually hit dead centre – in the paunch. That's why there wasn't much blood; the exit hole is occluded by skin movement. Under those circumstances it's better to wait at least half an hour for it to die, or at least stiffen up. Sometimes that is difficult. At all events, it must be painstakingly re-stalked with even more care than you would take with an unwounded animal. Having lost it, you must sink your pride and let people know round about – keepers and farm workers – in case they can spot it and ring you. Ideally, all stalkers should either have and train a dog to deer, or know whom to contact locally who can help. If you know you can get hold of a trained dog, don't tramp about too much at the site spoiling the scent before getting it, or the unfortunate hound is likely to be confused.

As the corn crops get higher, I am lucky if I can see more of a deer than the head. Is it best to try for a head shot, or guess where its body is and aim down to that?

Head shots taken from the side almost always result in a broken jaw, which is agonising, but not fatal in the short term. It is risky taking a shot at a deer's head, which is at the end of a long and mobile neck, here one second and licking itself the next. If the beast is looking away, or straight at you, and you are very close and sure of your shooting, that is more likely to kill it on the spot. Aiming off into the crop is pointless. You can't really tell where the vital organs might be, and in any case a bullet's path through growing vegetation is unpredictable. Did you know that a wheat field can stop machine gun fire? Often the best solution is a portable high seat which commands a much better and safer view for several more weeks before the crop is head-high. Try also to get the deer before they go out into the crops.

I am 55 and have been shooting since I was 17. I took up deer stalking in April this year as a member of a syndicate on a six thousand-acre forestry in Scotland. I was told there were substantial numbers of red and roe on this land. Although I have been out stalking some fifteen times I have only seen about twelve roe does, all of which were out of season, and no reds or bucks. I don't think I'm doing anything wrong; could I have been misled as to the amount of deer? As I am a novice, your comments would be appreciated.

Deer stalking in unfamiliar commercial conifer blocks is notoriously difficult and getting to know whether there really is a population of red and roe there has to be a two-pronged approach: looking for signs of occupation and going about actual stalking in the most productive way. As a deer consultant I have frequently had to make up my mind quickly about similar problems in the shortest order, being paid, as it were, by maximum results in a minimum time.

The first step is acute observation as you walk round: is there a browse line on ride-side trees? Is it one metre high (roe) or two metres (red)? Are any bushes browsed or frayed? (Note the height.) Is there a deer-trodden track inside any fences? If so – look for slots. Look for likely crossing points (racks) and where deer have slipped in crossing ditches. A visit to the local gunmaker or pub can also produce information. Local forest workers probably know a good deal.

Out stalking, work any stream sides; find open spaces where the winter sun strikes as it rises. When the midges are bad, investigate the highest ground. At all times have regard for the wind: it swirls maddeningly in any clearings. Failing a pipe or cigarette, try a child's bubble kit – it works!

When I take somebody out woodland stalking, should I perform the gralloch or can I leave it to him?

This does depend a bit on relations between stalker and visitor. When I took out paying guests as a professional, I felt it a duty to gralloch and to carry the beast back to the car, if a roe or muntjac, or otherwise deal with the carcass as part of the service. Some liked to deal with their own beasts, and that was fine by me, provided they were capable of producing an acceptable job. I learned my gralloching from an Austrian *Jager* who not only did a thorough job on a chamois carcass with surgical precision, but kept himself and his green uniform immaculate. Since then I have despised the grunting and heaving and general mess that some stalkers accept as normal.

If two amateurs go out together as host and guest, the host might feel obliged to offer to gralloch a beast shot by his guest, but equally the guest in turn should offer to do it, particularly if he happens to be younger. The exception in both cases is when there is a question of tuition. A novice stalker needs to be shown how to do a neat job by somebody more experienced, but after that he should get down to it with a bit of back-seat driving as needed from his tutor.

One can imagine occasions when the host, professional or otherwise, has to go off and collect transport from a distance. In that case he would be pleased if on his return he found the beast ready for collection, neatly cleaned. Less so if it had been haggled about. Some of my regular clients were not as accurate as I would have liked, either from excitement, an inclination to flinch due to over-gunning or a 'don't care' attitude provided the animal was dead somehow. For these I had a rule: gut-shot animals were gralloched by the client, regardless of professional ethics – and they knew it! One persistent offender had a word for it – if there was any likelihood of 'marmalade' because he had put a shot wrong, I left him to go ahead!

What is the best thing to do if one comes across an injured deer on the side of the road? I do a bit of stalking, but obviously don't carry a weapon in the car all the time. Anyway, there are likely to be people about. Should I phone the police, or try to find out who is the adjoining landowner – or just drive on and report it to someone?Now we know how many deer are killed in collisions, it's going to happen more and more.

It's something one dreads, and you need to have a few basic ideas to fit into the situation as you find it. Obviously if it's on a motorway you can't stop – just phone the police giving the location as near as you can, and the direction you are travelling.

On ordinary roads, if stationary vehicles are likely to make a traffic hazard, especially at night, it's as well to inform the police, putting your warning flashers on, preferably far enough away from the blockage to allow drivers to slow down. Some County forces have a list of people who are competent to deal with an injured beast. If you personally aren't very experienced don't try any amateur effort, especially if the public are present. If you call a vet, you may find yourself with a hefty bill. A stalker called out will probably have a powerful lamp, a stalking rifle or shotgun in case the animal is mobile, a .22 rifle which is now legal and is highly effective as a humane killer (after moving any onlookers safely out of the way), and a suitable knife. The most unobtrusive method of dispatching a deer is to bend its nose downward and thrust the knife down between the atlas and axis vertebrae just behind the ears to sever the spinal cord. This needs practice before using it on a live animal. If you are qualified to dispatch deer, I am assured that this is sufficient reason to carry a suitable knife in your car at all times in spite of current legislation demanding a reason for being in possession of one when not actively stalking.

A friend was told by the stalker when out after hinds this winter to head-shoot all his hinds as the venison dealer would not accept body-shot carcasses. This is a concern in itself, but in attempting a head shot from the front, his bullet glanced off the hind's forehead, at which the stalker took his rifle and downed it. Two questions: have you ever known a bullet glance off a deer's skull like that, and is this mandatory head-shooting justified?

No to both. Examples have been quoted to me of a bullet being deflected by the heavily built and steeply sloping skull of a wild boar in drives abroad, but it must be very rare indeed for a bullet from a stalking rifle to do the same on a hind without even stunning it.

Head-shooting is unfortunately something that younger stalkers tend to brag about, but for a game dealer to make that proviso is extraordinary and regrettable. Hind stalking has to go forward in all sorts of weather with the prime aim to achieve the cull with humanity and regardless of the weather. One can easily be tired and unsteady, deathly cold or trying to keep the rifle still in half a gale, none of these giving rifle-range precision.

The head of a deer is a very mobile object, turning this way and that without warning, and the lethal area, brain and spine, is very small indeed. The slightest error in shots from the side results in a broken jaw or a bullet through the nasal cavity, neither of them immediately fatal. Even from front or behind, the only shots remotely permissible in stalking terms, the head can move enough to result in a wound or miss. What might be allowable in park culling should not be enforced, especially on guest stalkers.

I am starting to take visitors out stalking in association with a local sporting agent. In the woods one can't walk two abreast, so should I go in front or behind the client?

This is a knotty one! If you come behind the client and you see a deer first (which is likely) he will go blundering on and nothing short of a shout will stop him. On the other hand if you go in front to get over that difficulty, you don't know where the muzzle of his rifle is pointing, or if he remembered to put the safety catch on again. That is an uncomfortable feeling. At the end of one such stalk, my client turned to me to find out how to unset the hair trigger! The thought of that rifle at my back, safety off and hair trigger set, haunted me for years. I prefer to see what's going on, even if a client marches on regardless occasionally. It is worth telling him before the stalk that you will say 'Stop' at the critical moment. That's less likely to scare a deer than hissing or whistling.

As a single-handed stalker I have a bit of difficulty with my paying guests. They always want to come two at a time. It's all right if one is an old client who I can trust to do what I say and go where I tell him, then I take out the other, but if I am uncertain of both, how does one cope without annoying them?

You are not alone with this dilemma! I can only tell you of my own attempt at a solution, which was to take the one I trusted least with me, putting the other in a high seat or possibly alternating between the two during their stay to make things fair.

The high-sitter was given some extremely strict rules, on penalty of being sent home. Most important – he was not allowed to leave the high seat until fetched. Safe and unsafe directions to shoot etc. were explained. Then I told him how to recognise the buck which he was allowed to take: principally the antlers, how far above the ears, some description of his points, age and other distinguishing marks. I would add that there was another buck in the vicinity, but that one was not for him under any circumstances. On the whole it worked well, but when staying with a party of regular clients in Belgium, one asked another 'Have you ever had these precise instructions before being put in a high seat?'

'Yes,' he replied. 'It was very impressive how well he knows his bucks.'

'And did Richard tell you there was another buck about?'

'Well, yes.'

'But did he ever describe the buck you *weren't* allowed to shoot?'

'Well, no!'

So don't try the same ploy with too many of your clients, or you will get rumbled like I did!

Many of us are stressed these days, and as a professional stalker I have seen too many guests reacting to the pressures of a week in the office by being as tense as wires and quite unable to relax and achieve that state of quiet attention which is vital to stalking success.

What actions do you suggest to cope with a guest who is like a cat on hot bricks?

Your own reaction is the first step to this all too common situation – the guest must be calmly but firmly handled. If he is led to understand his own problem it's a start, which of course begins at the zeroing range. No excuses, such as 'It is spot-on', 'I shot a leopard with it last week' or whatever – he must fire some rounds and if the results are appalling, show them to him. Don't let him cut things so tight that he arrives at the rendezvous with smoking tyres, making one last phone call on the way. Mobile phones are useful in an emergency but must be switched off at all times in the forest. Don't encourage talk on business or politics! Sleep must be made up, by totally banning any shopping or sightseeing trips with wives during the day, or even by sacrificing one or two early morning outings. If he walks too fast suggest an early start for the evening stalk, and to take the initial steam off take a long, preferably uphill, route where there are no deer. If that hasn't slowed him down, let him go in front and then stop while he disappears ahead. Tell him when he wanders back that there was a buck… if only he had stopped. That works!

You may feel you are behaving like Hitler, but either the client will respect your attitude in the end or he won't. In that case you don't need to have a spare week for him another time. That sort will only wound your animals, take dangerous shots and generally make your life a misery.

There was a good deal of local indignation last winter over a drive which was organised because of the numbers of muntjac in the woods. I know that deer drives used to take place but were effectively finished by the passing of the original Deer Act. However the sporting press and some recent books on deer management seem to condone what they refer to as 'moves'. Where is the line drawn between one and the other?

The old-style deer drives usually took the form of a back-end keepers' jolly, numbers often being made up with any volunteers who happened to own a shotgun even if it was not much used for the rest of the year. Woods were driven as if for pheasants. Shotguns were the accepted weapon and as a result many deer either escaped wounded or died without being found. Public opinion and the rise of the sport of woodland stalking reinforced the power of the law to see such drives recede into history.

Deer have increased in many parts of the country and controlling numbers depends on limiting the number of breeding females which has proved difficult in some places through legitimate stalking. Access to woodland through the game shooting season may be restricted which adds to the stalker's difficulties and one solution has been the development of the 'move'. In essence this consists of quietly moving the deer to one or more concealed riflemen. On one estate where I have taken part, only experienced stalkers are invited and very precise instructions are issued, the first of which is that *no shot should be taken at a moving deer*. The rifles are posted on high seats, mainly in woodland glades where the deer are likely to hesitate before running across the fields.

One or at most two 'walkers' then move quietly on pre-planned routes. All rifles are equipped with phones so that when the required cull is achieved, the move can be called off and culled animals collected.

The essential difference is therefore that a 'drive' involves trying to shoot frightened deer, and may continue even now under legal pretext and involve using shotguns, a situation that the British Deer Society has attempted to counter by proposing that shotguns are never allowed to be used to kill deer under any circumstances. Moves, when responsibly planned, do not involve any more risk of deer being wounded than from stalking.

The law and safety

Stalking has become hedged round with a mass of bureaucracy though which we have to tread much more warily these days. In addition the public are much more touchy, even if they are not actively opposed to shooting in general. One has to imagine a rambler, a birdwatcher, a camper lurking behind every bush night and day, and if not actually in danger, liable to be perturbed to an unexpected degree. The fact that they may be trespassing makes not a pick of difference. Nor must they fall out of your high seats without having been warned in writing of the unsuitability of such an action.

So one does not parade dead animals in the back of pick-ups, leave grallochs where loose dogs can retrieve them with pride to their owners, or dress Rambo-style in cammo gear hung about with visible knives. A sound moderator, though it may ruin the look or balance of your rifle, is a sound investment for most woodland stalkers.

Treating the beasts you shoot with respect is an area where we could learn from some other countries to our advantage. It is also necessary to remember that we are handling meat destined for human consumption, and if some of the hygiene regulations appear to have remote relevance to actual conditions on the hill or in the woods, nonetheless there is room for improvement even now. I did once ask an over-zealous Environmental Health Officer where I should conceal my white gumboots and waterproof apron when actually stalking, but he just thought I was being troublesome.

Underlying all this are two sets of Regulations, those concerned with Health and Safety and others with Meat Hygiene. All stalkers must be familiar with them, and many stalking situations demand that a formal Risk Assessment has to be prepared and kept up to date. These matters lie outside the scope of this book. They form an essential part of stalking courses leading to Level 1 and 2 qualifications, which every stalker should master. Helpful suggestions may also be found in these books:

Parkes C and Thornley J, *Deer: Law & Liabilities*, Quiller Press, 2008
Potter L, *Deer Stalking and Management*, Crowood Press, 2008
Prior R, *Roe Deer: Management and Stalking*, Swan Hill Press, 2006

I know that a shotgun should always be unloaded when crossing a fence etc., but with the greater safety of a bolt-action rifle, does the same apply to stalking?

The straight answer is YES. Every stalker should know about and take the various competence tests for woodland stalking. Just omit to unload faced with a fence to cross or a ditch to negotiate while in the practical exam and you will fail! Everyone needs to be shown, not least the passing public, that we are responsible and above all safe firearms users. A great deal can go wrong in the process of climbing up a high seat. Rungs can break; hit your head on the door lintel or slip on accumulated pigeon dung and you do a swallow dive. All moments when it is better not to have a cartridge in the breech or magazine.

Walking in the country is a major national pastime, as is birdwatching. Stalkers should never assume the woods are empty at any time of day or night.

A farmer has asked me to get rid of the foxes on his land because they are digging up his fields. Am I allowed to bury the carcasses?

I downloaded from the Defra website the document Animal Health and Welfare. Animal By-Products: Fallen Stock Questions & Answers. *In this it states 'The carcases, or part carcases, of wild animals are exempt from the scope of EU Animal By-Products Regulations unless they are thought to be diseased or used to produce game trophies.'*

I presume from this that it is therefore legal to bury any foxes that I shoot. Any comments regarding this matter would be of interest.

This useful exclusion is of vital interest not only to fox shooters but deer stalkers too, who need to bury offal and so on. It still needs to be done with considerable care so that it is not liable to be found and dug up by dogs or cause nuisance or distress to the public.

The situation is covered in that essential reference book for all stalkers, *Deer: Law and Liabilities* by Charlie Parkes and John Thornley. They state that the carcasses of all wild animals are exempt from the scope of the regulations with two exceptions: those suspected of being infected with a disease communicable to humans or animals, and deer whose bodies or parts of bodies are used to produced game trophies.

They go on to suggest that deer shot in the UK are shot primarily for their venison as part of a management plan, and therefore do not fall with the scope of the regulation.

Having got this out of the way, you still have somehow to explain to your farmer friend that the animals digging up his fields are much more likely to be badgers than foxes. A matter of some diplomacy which we all have to exercise when trying on one hand to sort out a misconception on the part of a landlord, but at the same time not risk the loss of one's sport.

What are the proposed changes in deer law? I gather that .22 centrefires are to be allowed for small deer, but not roe. What are your comments?

Basically these changes came into effect on 1 October 2007. Only England and Wales are affected:

- The open doe/hind season for all species except muntjac is extended by four weeks to the end of March.
- .22 centrefire rifles above certain limits (muzzle energy 1356 joules or 1000 ft/lbs) will be allowed for muntjac and Chinese water deer, but not for roe.
- Under licence from Natural England or Welsh Ministers, deer may be taken out of season and at night where other measures are not effective.
- Deer may be shot from a vehicle, provide it is stationary and the engine is not running.
- Shooting a dependent fawn/calf already or about to be deprived of its mother will be permitted.
- The humane dispatch of deer suffering as a result of illness or disease is allowed by any reasonable means.
- Imposes a close season for *all* Chinese water deer and hybrid red/sika female deer from 1 April to 31 October inclusive.

It is advisable to get full details of these changes, which can be found at http://www.opsi.gov.uk/si/si2007/ uksi 2007 2183 en.pdf
The title is *The Regulatory Reform (Deer) (England & Wales) Order 2007.*

Everyone will welcome the liberalisation of permitted weapons for the humane dispatch of sick deer, especially those involved in traffic accidents, and the close season for Chinese water deer is timely. It is to be hoped that the extension of the open season for female deer will only be used in situations where culling earlier in the season has not been possible, for example on intensive game shoots, and not just as an easy option. So far as the exclusion of roe from the .22 centrefire provisions, it is difficult to follow the argument against harmonising with Scotland, where no problems have arisen over legalising certain .22 centrefires for roe.

I can't find out whether it is legal to stalk deer on a Sunday. Nobody I have phoned gives a straight answer. Can you help?

There should be no question about this: you can shoot deer on a Sunday, assuming that otherwise you have the right. The Game Act 1831 specified that it is an offence for any person in England and Wales to kill or take *any game* on a Sunday or Christmas Day. The misunderstanding arises because at that time deer were not considered game, and were not included in the definition.

A parallel question arises over the letting (or retention) of 'the right to shoot game'. Because deer for many years were not regarded as game, they should be specifically mentioned in any agreement as being included or otherwise.

An exclusive right to kill game or deer may, however, leave the holder of the right liable for damage to crops etc. done by that particular species.

The position in Scotland is different in that there are no legal restrictions on shooting on Sundays, but there is a strong tradition that one should not do so. In fact all stalkers should be considerate about local feelings on this subject anywhere in the country. Sunday is a day set apart by many people on religious grounds and to others it is a day for quiet relaxation. Field sports are under the microscope these days and we must all do our utmost not to annoy others, or now everyone is terrorist-minded, give anyone cause for alarm either from loud gunshots or unnecessary displays of arms, clothing or dead game at any time, but especially on Sunday.

Although Game Licences have been abolished in England and Wales, you still need one to stalk deer on unenclosed land in Scotland.

I shot a deer which ran over my boundary into the middle of a field where it died. The landowner is claiming the carcass, but I had the stalking rights where it was standing when I shot it. Who is in the right?

The march – or boundary – has always been regarded as perilous ground and any stalker is well advised to talk things over with his neighbours and come to an agreement before such an event actually happens. The actual legal position in the case of deer is probably different from the case of a gamebird.

If Mr Smith legitimately shoots a pheasant over his own land and it falls *alive* on Mr Jones' land, though Smith has some claim on the bird and may feel morally obliged to pursue it, he commits a poaching offence if he retrieves the bird without Jones' permission. If Smith retrieves *dead* game from Jones' land which was in the first instance legitimately shot over his own land, he commits an act of civil trespass if permission is not sought to retrieve the game, even though Smith has a legal right to ownership of the game.

Deer are not game. In *Deer: Law and Liabilities* (Quiller, 2008 Edition) the authors state that the common law has always conveyed to the landowner certain rights in respect of the use of the land and things found upon it. Consequently deer found dead on the land, caught accidentally in fences *or killed in some other way* become the property of the landowner, subject to any legal agreement in which the rights may have passed to another – e.g. in a sporting lease.

The sensible course is to establish good relations with your neighbours from the start. If you haven't cleared this situation with them before it happens, then it would be prudent to make contact before making incursions on to other property, no matter how urgent it might be to end the suffering of an injured animal.

I don't seem to be able to find out whether there is a lower age limit for accompanied stalking. I am keen to introduce my son to deer stalking. Apart from the firearms laws, how old do you think a boy should be before he can be given a start? I could take him out on the hill, or low ground.

My usual reference, Parkes and Thornley's *Deer: Law and Liabilities* (Quiller, 2008) gives a slightly equivocal answer to this: 'Children under 14 cannot possess Section 1 firearms or ammunition. It is an offence to make a gift or lend a firearm to a child … unless he is carrying it for, and under the instruction of, the owner who is the holder of an appropriate certificate and using it for sporting purposes.'

However, my advice (and that of BASC) is that children under fourteen years cannot have access to, or use Section 1 firearms under any circumstances. Between fourteen and seventeen they may hold a firearms certificate and use the weapons specified, but can only acquire weapons and ammunition by gift or loan from a certificate holder.

Quite apart from the precise legal situation, I would suggest that there are other considerations when introducing young people to stalking. Every father wants to see his children sharing his hobbies, and too often their interest can be killed rather than kindled by having 'too much, too early'. Too often over-keenness on the father's part is the best way to breed a life-time aversion. So the straight answer is – only let him come when he is desperate to go with you! The attention span of a child tends to be short, and they soon get bored and cold. Success is vital, so choose a nice day and take him where you are sure to see deer. A deer park or wildlife centre may be as good a start as any. Show them to him, teach him how to use the binoculars – and go home. Then wait for the idea to breed and grow. When he is even keener than you are – that is the moment, not before, but it must always be a rare treat and a privilege.

Any rifle legal for deer has a substantial recoil. This and the weight of the weapon may be discouraging, even for a well-grown boy. A flinch developed at this stage can haunt anyone for years, and should a deer be wounded the experience could put any young person off completely. One should also consider the welfare of the deer against the excitement and consequent lack of accuracy which would be more than understandable in the circumstances. Take him out by all means and teach him the ways of deer and stalking, but regard taking a shot as a prize after reaching the legal age, and having been able to show on the range that precise shooting is not only achievable, but maintained under pressure.

I have been stalking a bit of ground for years with a very informal arrangement, just taking the occasional beast. I've never bothered with trophies, it's the stalking I enjoy, with some venison to eat. Now my landlord's son is taking over and inevitably is looking to let the stalking at prices I can't think about.

Have I just got to look round for somewhere else, or have you any advice about coping with the situation?

If you do manage to find some new ground locally, even between friends it is prudent to have a definite written agreement. Besides any question of security of tenure, it does give you a definite status as an occupier (of the stalking rights) which can be important nowadays. Also stalking has an increasing value, and maybe it's a good idea to offer at least a nominal rent even if you and the owner both feel that you are performing a service to the farm or estate.

With a 'new broom' on your familiar stalking, it may be worth talking things over before abandoning ship completely. Point out that only the bucks have a trophy value and unless he wants to deal with the rest of the cull himself, he or the lessee might be glad to leave the does and yearlings to you. At least part on good terms. Quite often high-rent stalking agreements end after a season or two, and the owner may be glad to welcome you back!

Whenever I go stalking I get covered with ticks crawling up my legs and elsewhere. What is the best method of getting them off, and is there any way of stopping the invasion?

Ticks need a drink of blood before each stage of their life cycle, and crawl up the herbage when it is moist, where they wait for a potential host to pass. Putting out a hooked claw, they come on board. The worst collector of ticks is the traditional breeches stocking. Trousers are less of a magnet. When the ticks are bad, tuck your trousers into your boots.

You may also pick ticks up from carrying or dressing deer. They are active from late spring to autumn. Besides various animal diseases, they carry at least one disease which you need to know about. If a tick bite develops into a red spot larger then a 10 pence piece, go and see your GP and mention Lyme disease. It has been suggested that something like 30 per cent of our tick population are now carriers of the disease.

The current entry in Wikipedia suggests that the longer the tick is attached, the worse the risk of infection. Also that some methods of removal may make the tick regurgitate its stomach contents into the host, including the infective agent, so, as it says, the tick should not be 'disturbed'! They suggest gripping it with tweezers as near the head as possible, and pulling straight off, no twisting. The area should be disinfected with alcohol or hydrogen peroxide. As an alternative, take a length of sewing cotton, make a thumb knot and tighten this loop round the parasite close to your skin. Pulling both ends will then dislodge the tick.

One can get a handy removal tool which appears to do much the same job from Bushwear (0845 226 0469). They also market 'Tick Pliers', tick removal patches and some deterrent liquids.

This concerns my son now aged seventeen. Ever since he could walk he has accompanied me stalking. When he was about eleven I asked him to drag a roe deer to the edge of a field for collection; it was then he complained of a rash on his hands and arms, puffy eyes, wheezing and sneezing – at the time I put it down to hay fever. As he got older he started to shoot roe and the problem got worse,

He now will not touch one, as the symptoms can last up to three days. He has tried anti-histamine after the event but the symptoms persist, even one hair on the back of his hand will produce a rash, similar to nettle rash. He suffers from hay fever in the summer, but apparently has no other allergies. He can handle both fallow and muntjac with no problems; he works with horses, and is in contact with dogs and cats and other farm animals on a regular basis. Have you heard of this before? If so what can be done to stop these very distressing symptoms, which occur all the year round? I would be most grateful for any suggestions or help you can offer.

Obviously your son needs advice from an allergy specialist. I can sympathise as I have suffered similarly all my professional life. At first it was only deer (it is surprising if he is only allergic to roe) but later horses, cattle, cats and dogs affected me. Even standing downwind of a deer herd produced asthma. It appeared to be cumulative – the more exposure, the worse it got. As deer were my career I could not do the obvious thing and immediately take an office job, so in conjunction with advice from my GP and specialists I took avoidance action in the form of gloves and anti-histamine both internally and as cream on my hands, and at times put on an industrial mask when handling deer. I kept a nebuliser with me at all times, and took steroids when they were prescribed. Individuals of course vary and allergies are better understood these days. Your son must be guided by those better qualified than me.

The land agent for the estate where I stalk tells me that I must submit a 'risk assessment' and put warning notices on my high seats because of the Health and Safety Regulations. I do the deer control for nothing, so if I tell him I will be responsible, do I have to go through all this nonsense?

I'm afraid you do. You and the agent have a responsibility under these regulations which you can't avoid. In addition, your seats must be properly designed and be formally inspected (with a report to the estate in writing) twice a year. This is modern stalking. It is a complicated subject which is summarised for stalkers in my book *Roe Deer: Management and Stalking* (Swan Hill Press, 2006). There is also an extended section on the subject in Lewis Potter's *Deer Stalking and Management* (Crowood Press, 2008).

A red stag has been a resident in my local park for fourteen months. When he arrived the stag was very shy and would not appear until late dusk or you could catch a glimpse of him at dawn before he disappeared back into the scrub or the bulrushes. When he arrived I made a point of trying to glass him on many an evening, but now I see him at least twice a week without the need of binoculars. The park in question is very popular with local dog walkers, cyclists and families; on some Sundays well over one thousand people can visit the area over the period

High seats need to be inspected twice a year and have a warning notice against unauthorised use.

of the day. My concern is that the red stag is not as shy as he used to be and from December last year he has become very bold and chases the horses away from their feeding areas to get his fill of hay. He can be seen throughout the day and has become a local talking point, standing his ground if a unruly dog gets too close. During the rutting period last year he was still in his shy/unsure period and I expressed some concern to the park workers that he could possibly become dangerous. He is a solitary male with no other red deer in the park.

It is so pleasing to the eye to see an animal of this grandeur from a safe distance, but yesterday I was walking my four Labradors off the lead to heel when the stag presented himself to me no more than ten metres in front. It was clear he was not going to move. I made eye contact and walked backwards along the public footpath. I kept walking backwards for fifty metres and then turned to walk in the normal manner. What if a small child was put in the same position as myself and the stag was having a 'bad day'?

My question is do you think this environment is suitable? I have over thirty-five years experience of game shooting and stalking. I would like to pass your comments on to the park manager.

As you appreciate, a red stag accustomed to people and therefore not afraid of them is potentially a dangerous animal at all times of the year and especially so during the rut. The fact that he has no hinds probably exaggerates the problem. My advice to the warden is that there is a considerable risk to park users from this situation. As soon as is practicable the stag should either be tranquillised and removed, or destroyed before someone gets hurt.

With the present debate in the North about abolishing any close season for male deer, one wonders if there are really good reasons for it, or if this is part of an anti-deer undercurrent, wherever that comes from. My own feeling is that there must be both practical and ethical reasons for shooting deer when they are in hard horn, but I find difficulty in putting them straight in my mind. Would you please give me your opinion on these two points?

One has to start with the notion that it doesn't make any difference to a deer whether it is shot in hard horn or at any other time of year. However, I personally find the idea of killing stags or bucks when they are shed or in velvet repugnant unless there are over-riding reasons for it. For most of us shooting a heavily pregnant female is worse. This is a question of sporting ethics and sadly the proposal on the abolition of a close season has nothing to do with sport but is the result of a conflict of interests within multiple land use.

Where I do see very cogent reasons for restricting the shooting of male deer to a period when females need protection because of dependent young is this: in the months when females can properly be shot, the days are short, the weather often appalling and with the added complication in many places of conflict with other activities, such as game shooting, hiking, winter sports and so on, the achievement of a full cull becomes arduous and difficult. Yet the truth has to be faced, no matter what side you take in the reduction of numbers argument that *the only way of reducing the breeding herd of any animal is to reduce the number of females.*

It follows that if in the period you can legitimately cull females you waste time by taking males, that action defeats the whole object.

I often visit deer parks open to the public to try for photos. Some of the deer are pretty tame, and I wonder if there are any risks attached? Now that there even have been some accidents with cows, ought one to be careful?

Yes. Deer are large, strong animals, and the less fear they have of humans, the more potential risk exists for personal injury, intentional or otherwise. I have several times been horrified to see adults encouraging children to approach or even feed park deer.

Park deer lose their fear of man and may become dangerous, especially in the rut. The public should be warned against attempting to feed them or get too near at any time

103

Much depends on the species involved and the time of year. All male deer get steamed up with adrenalin in the run up to and during the rut and need especial care at that time. Red stags in particular are definitely dangerous when rutting and should not be approached. While any deer is in hard horn a toss of the head, maybe just to dislodge a fly, could quite accidentally inflict serious injury on anyone close by. Tame roebucks, in spite of their small size, have a poor reputation, and can turn quite savage, particularly to women, as several owners of 'rescued' fawns have found to their cost. Fallow deer have the cleanest bill of health in this respect and accidents attributed to this species are rare. However, in *The Mammals of Great Britain and Ireland*, J G Millais recorded that a fatal accident occurred in Greenwich Park in November 1905. 'An unfortunate hairdresser named Sadler was reading a newspaper in the park when he was suddenly attacked by a buck which inflicted such serious injuries that he died a few days afterwards in the Seamen's Hospital.' Surprisingly this incident was outside the normal rutting time – so it pays always to treat park deer with respect.

An incident has been reported recently of a beater on a pheasant day knocked down by a roe doe and seriously injured. As I beat regularly myself, I wonder how often incidents like this happen and whether there is any advice which you can give me?

To answer your first question, the likelihood of a deer knocking somebody down is fairly remote, but it does happen from time to time and if the deer is large or an antlered male, then the results can be serious indeed. Obviously any deer caught in a covert being driven will try to escape and usually does without problems. However, if cornered or panicked it will flee blindly and then an accident can happen.

The best advice is what *not* to do! There does tend to be a bit of excitement in the beating line when a deer is roused, plus some bad language if it starts a big flush. If it is greeted by loud shouts or even, as I have seen, the man most concerned behaving as if he were driving cattle, waving his arms and bawling, then the deer is understandably frightened, puts down its head and charges anybody in the way.

So in deer country, and that's most of Britain, *don't* shout or demonstrate, let it leak out on its own path. If a deer should rush the line, throw yourself out of its path or at worst lie down. A hoof in the back is better than an antler in the stomach.

We have masses of muntjac which the local stalkers seem unable to control. They are a real pest, eating our bluebells and checking coppice growth. They are a nuisance on shooting days too, running about ahead of the beaters and flushing birds in droves. Admittedly much of our woodland is thick and difficult to stalk. Also there are two main roads and some housing development adjoining which limits the use of deer rifles in part of the estate. Using the exemptions contained in the Deer Act we are entitled to use shotguns to control muntjac and this may be the only option. However, I gather there are moves afoot to ban the shotgun totally regardless of the circumstances. Do you approve of this?

I have campaigned for decades against the use of shotguns for deer; however, one has to look at the facts objectively.

The paramount need is to exercise all deer control in as humane a manner as possible and this has always been the prime aim of the anti-shotgun crusade. Anyone who is old enough to have witnessed the results of the lamentable shotgun deer drives which used to be a normal event in February would recoil from any prospect of going back to that, but the deer concerned were red, fallow, sika and roe. Nothing can shift my determination that a suitable rifle and ammunition is the only weapon for humane use against such large animals.

Muntjac have spread widely, and are a growing concern because of the damage they are capable of inflicting on the flora, such as orchids and bluebells, on the natural regeneration of broadleaved woodland and on coppice regrowth. They flourish in thick undergrowth where they are difficult to see, and have penetrated into urban environments where the use of a deer rifle is out of the question.

The current interest in stalking muntjac is to be encouraged but has not stemmed the tide of colonisation or prevented muntjac densities building up in places to an unacceptable level. The frequency of traffic accidents involving these deer is an indicator of how many there are about. Most stalkers with experience of the species will admit that it is a very challenging sport not only because of the small size of the beasts, but from their habit of continuously wandering about. The skill and excitement of stalking them needs to be taught more widely. Eventually legitimate shooting pressure may be enough to limit the population. However, the present situation on many estates is a muntjac population only limited by their territoriality, and causing damage and conflict with other activities.

We now have deer management qualifications, which did not exist until recently. I feel that where rifle control is clearly not enough, qualified deer managers should have a mandate to make use of the shotgun and suitable ammunition and carry out small-scale moves to offer close-range shots. The most effective shot size is probably BB. The very large shot sizes now sanctioned by the Deer Act under certain conditions produce poor patterns and have a dangerous tendency to ricochet. At the time of the original Deer Act in 1963, tests showed that anything larger than AAA stacked poorly in a 12-bore but this size was selected as the *largest* possible because it was being allowed for the big deer species. In the controlled circumstances suggested, and especially in urban and suburban surroundings, shot larger than BB could be dangerous.

Conditions for authorising these muntjac control exercises could readily be devised to limit abuse. We must lay down practical guidelines before the situation becomes even worse. A total ban under present circumstances is inappropriate.

6 Kit

Ever been caught with a dead beast and no knife? One lady stalker of my acquaintance found herself in this position, so she beat out the empty cartridge case with a stone to make an edge and gralloched her stag with that. Admiring her resourcefulness, nonetheless it must be better to be properly equipped.

A stalker needs to be comfortable, unstressed and equipped with what he needs to do the job – neither more nor (especially) less – to enjoy his sport to the full. This needs a certain amount of thought and attention to detail. Nobody else is going to do it for you, that's one of the pleasures of woodland stalking. Even if you go out with somebody, either as a professional guide or a companion, he will expect you to have kitted yourself out properly and to have everything needed to hand. Don't be like one of my clients who, faced with a shootable buck, had not dared to load his rifle without my direct order and couldn't remember in which of many hidden pockets he had secreted his ammo!

Clothing needs to be multi-layered so that you can add or discard. Whatever finishes on the outside must be subdued in colour, rain-proof and not liable to make game-scaring noises when scraped by twigs. Reserves and cast-offs may be stored in the roe sack. Gloves are good to hide the flash of your hands when lifting the binoculars; boots must be light but waterproof – not a problem since the introduction of Gore-Tex and similar fabrics.

Rising early leads to hurry and things can too easily get left behind. Laying out what you need the night before is sensible. Although the rifle has to stay in safe storage until the last minute, put the sleeve out with the rest to act as a reminder. I find a short list of essentials a good safeguard against leaving something vital behind in the half-awake rush.

It may seem like tempting Providence when success seems pretty far away to have everything ready for when you do actually shoot something. However, if you don't, there's going to be a right mess. The small deer – roe and muntjac – are reasonably portable but remember the Great Public and also the Health Inspector! Carrying a carcass round your neck may be a sort of macho thing, but suddenly appearing on a footpath looking like Herne the Hunter will give an immediate attack of conniptions to the average hiker or birdwatcher. You are going to eat what you shoot – so be as hygienic as possible. Quite apart from public relations, the Demon Health and Safety insists that you don't strain yourself by heaving large deer about, so proper lifting gear and handling equipment need to be organised. There was a rumour that one large organisation had sent out an instruction to its stalkers that once shot, no deer weighing more than so many kilos was to be moved. However, no advice was given about lifting up the carcass in order to weigh it – and so discover whether it could be lifted. One of the many quagmires of bureaucracy.

Besides the basics of rifle, ammo, binoculars and stick, a collection of accessories adapted to your stalking needs can mean the difference between satisfaction and utter misery.

STALKER'S REMINDER LIST

Rifle, bolt, sling, scope, sound moderator.
Ammunition – in two rattle-proof pouches.
Roe sack, not less than 60 cm x 50 cm, plus waterproof liner.
Stalking jacket, boots. Calls, on a string to go round your neck.
Binoculars.
Stalking stick, bipod.
Hat, gloves or mittens. Midge veil and anti-midge cream.
Money. Mobile phone. Compass and map. Thermos. Money.
Rubber gloves. Knife and a reserve in the roe sack.
Small torch. Rope and string. Folding saw.
Poly bags, paper, pencil. Toilet paper, Band aid.
Spare handkerchief. Firearms Certificate.

I am planning to buy a rifle for roe and red deer but am unsure what calibre to get to ensure a clean kill on a red deer, but not to cause excessive damage to roe. What would you recommend?

There is a rather widespread fallacy that the bigger the calibre of a deer rifle, the more damage it does to the meat. Not so. In fact this has much more to do with a combination of speed and bullet design. Speed produces hydraulic shock which is transmitted from the bullet channel via the fluid-filled tissues, rupturing blood vessels and producing a hammer-like blow to the heart and nervous system – and doing damage in the process. Bullets for sporting use are designed first to penetrate and then to deform in order to transfer energy to the target quarry. Very light bullets, such as are designed for small vermin, are likely to expand or fragment immediately on a deer, creating a surface wound which damages a great deal of meat but may not be immediately fatal due to the lack of penetration. Too hard a bullet is likely to pass through a beast, still retaining and wasting much of its energy on the other side, and leaving such a small exit hole that it occludes, preventing a tell-tale blood trail. For large beasts penetration has to be deeper before the planned deformation takes place, hopefully in the vital area. So you have a choice: either select a calibre for which a variety of bullet weights are readily available, or select one for which standard loads are equally suitable for all deer, from muntjac to red stags. Luckily bullet makers are very clever at designing missiles which give fair expansion and adequate penetration. It does not pay to go too small – a big red stag in the height of the rut charged up with adrenalin takes a lot of stopping and the same applies to sika stags too. Although many stalkers use the .243 Winchester with 100-grain bullets even for these two, my own experience inclines towards something heavier. Besides, not all shots can be relied on to be ideally placed.

Getting supplies of cartridges easily (or cases if you are going to load your own) puts the 'fancy' calibres out. I have had satisfactory service for all species out of two old designs, the 7 × 57 (.275 Rigby) using 140-grain bullets and the .30-06 using 130 grain. The .308 Winchester suits short-action rifles and has a wide variety of bullet weights. Otherwise in your position I would look carefully at the 6.5 × 55 Swedish Mauser with 139-grain bullets. It has much to recommend it and is even allowed for elk in Scandinavia.

I have a super vari-power scope on my stalking rifle and don't see the reason for toting a big pair of binos (let alone buying them) when I can see everything with tremendous clarity through the scope. I got hauled over the coals by a professional stalker the other day, and felt a bit aggrieved, specially as he only had a pair of cheap 8 × 30s. Isn't this just a fad?

Just stop to think a minute – what is happening when you look at something through your scope? You don't take it off the rifle, so what you are doing is aiming a loaded rifle at an unidentified object, which may be a deer … or a dog … or a birdwatcher. *Don't.* Apart from that, a decent pair of binoculars will increase your enjoyment of the outing. Stalking isn't all wanting to shoot something. For woodland stalking I prefer a magnification of 7 × with object lenses around 40 mm. This gives you very fast use without too much need to adjust the focus. For open-hill stalking, unless you use a telescope, there are advantages in a variable or 10 × magnification so that you can make out the details of a stag or hind without having to approach very near it.

I learned my woodland stalking with a professional who always seemed to be able to get his vehicle pretty near anything we shot. A few yards' drag, heave it up and off home. Now I have some roe stalking of my own, mostly hill ground, and I am puzzled about the best way of getting them back. Can you help?

I have always used a rucksack (or roe sack) to tote my roe. Get a good big one (60 cm × 50 cm minimum), with a removable washable lining. After gralloching, fold the roe up with its head between its legs and dump it bottom-first into the lining. Then the whole package can be put in the roe sack without messing it up. The legs can stick up, but don't let the head dangle or it will drip over everything.

For deer up to roe size, a stout rucksack with a waterproof liner is ideal.

Humping a sika is a job for a strong man. A stumble might lead to back trouble, let alone getting spiked by the antlers.

I own a Blaser rifle which I wouldn't change for anything, but I am in a dilemma on calibre choice. I have a .22-250 for fox control and .243 Winchester for up to and including roe.

I have some farmland stalking in Somerset with small woods scattered about. Mostly roe but some fallow and muntjac. I use a .308 Winchester. Half the time shots are at pretty long range where one may have to crawl into range, but in the copses it's short-range work where one has to be quick, especially with the munts. Do you recommend a stick (maybe two tied together) or a bipod? Or just take regulation prone shots in the fields?

Personally, I have always used a tall stick, length up to eye level. This will give you the height and stability to shoot in and over cover in the woods. It is pretty quick if you carry it in your left hand (assuming you are right-handed) slinging the rifle on your right shoulder, muzzle down. It can be brought up to the shoulder with the minimum of movement and your left hand, holding the stick with three fingers, is ready to receive the fore-end. The natural way to hold a rifle for an off-hand shot is somewhat across the body to the left (for a right-hander). If your feet and the stick are more or less in line, you will have no lateral stability and wild shooting is the result. To use a stick effectively you need to stand rather more square-on, so that your two feet and the stick form a triangle on the ground, 'the basic tripod'. A split stick does help, but is slower in use and the two halves can rattle together at awkward moments. Dry practice at home is very helpful is developing a secure stance without having to think about it.

Out in the fields there is so often enough straw, growing crop or stones to make a classic prone shot impossible. A bipod with telescoping legs is invaluable for this sort of work, but they are slow and click loudly as you pull out the legs, so it is only helpful for long shots. One can get a long-legged version which gives a steady sitting position. For a deliberate shot in the open you are likely to have enough time to get the bipod out of your roe sack and clip it to the rifle. I prefer the sort which allow you to correct for tilt without fiddling with the legs.

When I go out stalking, how many rounds should I have with me? I always seem to go out weighed down with ammo looking like a bandit, and then if I'm lucky I get one shot. What do you do?

I sympathise, but one just has to allow for times when things go wrong. Also for what you expect to be doing. In the summer buck-stalking you probably hope for the one, but a good morning's doe culling in the winter might account for three – or half a dozen if the size of the cull and means of transport allow. The same thing applies on the hill. Every stalker, too, if he is truthful, has the occasional disaster no matter how careful they are with their shots. A wounded animal may require more than one shot to stop it, and stopping it should be only second to safety in deciding what you do.

The situation has changed a bit recently, as one is no longer allowed to leave a few rounds reserve in the car for emergencies, and few of us live so near our stalking that we can dash back to the house in case of need.

While I worked as a professional I had a leather case with ten rounds in it in my pocket, plus another with six which lived in the roe sack. For stags on the hill, just the ten never left me short.

I have what is called a non-slip sling on my stalking rifle, but it has to be hitched up all the time to stop it falling off, specially if I have the roe sack on. Is there any cunning way I can stop it?

Basically your trouble is not the rifle sling, but the rucksack straps, because even if your sling doesn't slip off the leather strap, it drags strap and all off your shoulder. Two stages to get over the difficulty: first sew a very small button on to the shoulder of your stalking jacket just below where the sling or roe sack strap sits comfortably. Not too big, otherwise the sling will hitch up when you want to get it unslung quickly. Second: glue some felt or similar non-slip material to that part of the roe strap. Motor factors sell a rubberised material made to stop items sliding about in the car. A strip of that glued on to the under and top side of the rucksack strap, and on the underside of the rifle sling, should work wonders.

I take care to protect my hearing when I'm out with the gun, using ear plugs, or muffs for clay pigeon shooting, but what do I do about stalking? One can't in practical terms prowl about the woods with muffs on, and the plugs would stop my hearing the sounds of deer moving etc. Are just a few shots a year going to do any damage? I am 26.

This is quite a problem every stalker should consider. It's not just the rifle's hearing that is at risk but anyone with him (including his dog) and especially the professional lying next to him as is so often the case on the open hill. I believe that *every* shot which you take unprotected has an effect on your hearing, but the damage is unlikely to show until you are in your 40s. Short-barrel rifles and any fitted with muzzle brakes are the worst offenders.

Taking the easiest problem first: always ensure that your dog is firmly sat behind you when you take a shot. A friendly animal may wander round to the front, if only to lick your face! For standing shots, it must be firmly at heel, not beside your feet. It's a sad fact that old dogs do get deaf, so don't hasten the process.

For every zeroing session, use your muffs and ensure that any nearby onlooker has them on too. Out stalking, you may have the time to put in your earplugs before a deliberate shot, but I doubt you will remember in the heat of the moment. I agree that non-electronic protectors would certainly inhibit a woodland stalker and the electronic sort are expensive. Those which are fitted to your ears are, of course, extremely effective, not only for stalking but for game shooting too. If you only have a very few shots a year, you may feel that won't do material harm, but more than this and you must weigh the cost against future deafness. I didn't know the risks, and am nearly stone deaf in the left ear as a result!

The alternative is to have your rifle fitted with a sound moderator. Besides other advantages, shooting with one is kinder on the ears. All Forestry Commission stalkers have to use one these days.

Last November I gralloched a sika stag and while doing it, grazed my finger. Later it swelled up, and the adjoining one too. I was prescribed antibiotics which reduced the swelling after a time but are there any particular poisons or diseases which I might have picked up?

Everyone knows that a stag, red or sika, smells awful during and after the rut but in the excitement of a successful shot it is easy to forget that we are trying to produce food fit for human consumption under somewhat adverse conditions, to put it mildly.

Stags *soil*, that is wallow, in a mud bath. The first effect is to blacken their coat and thus appear larger and more formidable to an adversary. They urinate in the wallow, and on themselves, so that they are covered by a stinking layer of mud and manure. One imagines that this may be attractive to the females he wishes to lure onto his rutting stand, no matter how vile it may be to our noses. Any open cut or abrasion lays a stalker open to a fairly noxious cocktail of infectious agents. In addition if he is unlucky enough to have an allergy to deer hair or blood he will suffer more than he usually would through breathing in the fumes.

So of course you did right to get medical help, and it is unlikely that there will be any long-term effects. The significant deer-associated Lyme disease is not spread by contact but by tick-bite, and while isolated cases of other diseases such as TB are reported from time to time, training in proper gralloching techniques should have warned the stalker to look out for suspicious abnormalities.

Rudimentary first-aid for cuts should be carried. A temporary but quite effective dressing can be improvised from a clean handkerchief, a polythene bag and a strip of adhesive plaster to keep it in place until something better can be done with a kit in the car.

On the open hill there is usually a stream handy in which one can wash, but not in woodland. Both for protection and in the name of hygiene it is advisable to wear gloves during the gralloch. I favour reasonably strong domestic rubber gloves rather than medical examination gloves which tear easily in the rough work of handling a heavy beast. I took to using these a long time ago for stalking in our dry chalk country. Well I remember the look of horror on the face of one of my Continental visitors when I produced a pair of yellow gloves. It quite spoiled my image as a *waidgerechter Jäger*!

How or with what do you sharpen the gut hook on a stalking knife as I have a sharp blade and blunt hook so only half a tool?

Sharpening your gut hook can be solved with a round section carborundum stick, or a slip stone which is wedge-shaped with rounded sides – coarse to start with, then fine grain to finish. Alternatively use a diamond-impregnated hone of the right contour. The same applies to those very handy little curved knives with a protected point which are so useful for skinning without puncturing or slitting the meat.

Here in Scotland we use .22 centrefires for roe (I favour the .222) but can you clear up an argument with a friend who wants to stalk south of the border? He wants to use lightweight bullets in handloads for his .243. Is this legal?

The legal position is quite clear: rifles for red, fallow, sika or roe deer in England and Wales have to have a minimum calibre of .240 inch and the ammunition must have a muzzle energy of not less than 1700 ft/lbs. The bullet must not be non-expanding, therefore hollow-point, soft nose and ballistic-tipped bullets are all legal. For muntjac and Chinese water deer the minimum calibre is .220 inches with a muzzle energy of not less than 1000 ft/lbs, bullet weight 50 grains minimum.

I am personally an admirer of the .222 for roe; its 50-grain bullet is well designed for the modest velocity generated by this cartridge, but it would be a great mistake for your friend to use ultra-light bullets in his .243 for the purpose. They are designed for vermin and do not have the penetration to be effective on roe, even if the nominal ballistics match up to English legal requirements. Most of my professional life as a stalker I used the .243, using 100-grain bullets of various makes. Some stalkers use the 90 grain. I would not suggest that he goes lower than this.

I do a lot of my stalking in semi-suburbia. Would a silencer be a good idea on my rifle? I gather one cannot eliminate the crack of a high-speed bullet.

There are a number of advantages in fitting a silencer (sound moderator). The noise is very much reduced, though there is still, as you suggest, a crack. From the point of view of people living close by, or working in the vicinity, the stalker's activities are less obtrusive, which is important these days. There may be nervous domestic livestock nearby which one is anxious not to frighten. In addition, if it is necessary to take more than one deer out of a group, as is often the case with does, the survivors of the first shot react very much less and may have difficulty in locating the source of the bang.

The main snags, of course, are added weight and the change in balance and handling of your rifle. A long-barrelled weapon might benefit from judicious shortening. Provided the moderator is fitted by a competent riflesmith and the manufacturer's instructions about maintenance are followed, accuracy is not affected.

The other point, which anyone is bound to feel who looks on his rifle as a work of art wedded to utility, is the loss of its looks. Maybe we sacrificed them long ago when scope sights started to be accepted as standard. Only the Lloyd rifle made any attempt to integrate rifle and scope into one design. When push comes to shove, one's rifle is primarily a tool which should be as efficient as modern technology can make it. Under the conditions you describe, any artistic reservations on design should give way to serving the stalker to the utmost in the task he has to perform.

I notice when I take shooting guests down to the range 'to try their rifles' (but mainly to inform the professional stalker as to their abilities) that many of them flinch. Some even shut their eyes when they pull the trigger! How can one tactfully get over this problem?

Flinching is a rifleman's bugbear. The origin may be the result of using an ill-fitting rifle (short stock, scope sight too near the eye), heavy recoil, or plain buck-fever. I developed a flinch some years ago when a series of primers blew back and it has been hard to cure. The only solution is to convince the flincher of his fault, of which he may be entirely unaware. One way is to hand him an unloaded rifle on the range which he thinks is ready to fire. The ensuing wave of the barrel when he pulls the trigger without a round in the chamber will be all too clear to everyone. If he is not prepared to take remedial action, all you can do is restrict him to shots from a high seat, or at very close range.

The proper way of going about it is to go back to the .22 RF, preferably using short ammunition with its negligible noise and recoil, and bang away until the habitual flinch is once again under control. It may take several boxes of cartridges! Anyone who recognises the symptoms in himself would be well advised to review his choice of rifle. There's no need to use 'too much gun' – all legal deer rifles have plenty of power *if the bullet goes into the right place*. Recoil is not only related to the chosen cartridge, though that of course is a prime cause. A short or poor-fitting stock may be doing the mischief, or that classic mistake may be at the bottom of the problem – choosing a rifle in the showroom 'because it is so delightfully light to carry'. I once knew a sexy little Mauser in 7 × 57 which weighed no more than a good .22. Delightful to carry and handle, it kicked like a mule. Another cause of uncomfortable recoil is excessive headspace – that is the clearance between bolt head and cartridge. This is something which needs to be checked by a qualified riflesmith.

The alternative, if you aren't fussy about appearances, is to fit a moderator. Just a very loud report can influence a shooter's steadiness, and with a moderator there is a noticeable reduction in recoil.

What is the best range to zero my rifle for woodland stalking? Part of the time I'm in thick cover and the ranges are short, but then there are deer out in the fields which involves longer shots. I use a .243 with 100-grain bullets. Most shots are at fairly short range. What is your advice about zeroing? Should I target spot-on at 100 yards, or lift the group an inch or more?

Look at the ballistic data for your load, which is usually printed on the back of each box. With the rifle zeroed spot-on at 100 yards I would expect the drop at 200 to be about three inches. That's enough to scruff or miss one of your field deer if you take a spot-on aim for the heart, taking a bit of excitement and the difficulty of accurate range estimation into account. I personally like to zero about an inch up for the conditions you describe, maybe aiming up a trifle on the beast for a long shot. This setting improves your chances at long but reasonable ranges, without leading to high shots on deer in the woods when there often isn't too much time to think about aiming down.

If you up the zero to make allowance for an over-optimistic shot towards 250 yards you will shoot too high in cover.

Stalkers tend to boast about the long shots they have brought off, but remember – you may be able to see the beast clearly enough at extended range, but set up a target sometime at that distance and see how far your bullets spread! When in doubt – don't! Those old elephant hunters had a saying 'Get really close – then ten yards closer!' Deer aren't dangerous game, but they still deserve to be treated with respect, not just as targets.

My stalking is part of our farming operations, so the rifle is mostly parked behind the seats of the Land Rover, where it has to take its chance of bumps and bangs. Clearly the scope is the most delicate part of the setup, so would it be better to have removable mounts, so that I can put it somewhere safer and only clip it on when it is needed?

I have seen some remarkably tough vibration tests at the Zeiss factory to which every scope manufactured is subjected – so fierce that the concrete plinth the test machine was mounted on literally shook. A good-quality scope can take some banging about without shaking its lenses loose. Often loss of zero is attributable to one of two things: uneven contact between barrel and fore-end or loose scope mounts. The more solid the mounts and the less they are moved, the better.

Many rifles made in Europe have claw-and-clip type mounts, allowing the scope to be taken off easily. However, even if they are very carefully machined, as is usually the case, repeated use can produce wear and lost movement which is fatal to accuracy. Dirt can also lodge in the slots with the same result. I had some very expensive twist-off mounts on one of my rifles, and even with those a test showed considerable tolerance which explained my disappointment with the weapon. Leave your scope on, and take a bit of trouble to protect it. If your rifle has a free-floating barrel, that is, it has no contact with the woodwork ahead of the chamber, or one where the forward end of the barrel is supported but with the rest clear of the fore-end, dirt, leaves etc. can build up in the channel, which is fatal to a consistent zero.

There is enough room behind the seats of a cab-type Land Rover or similar vehicle to have either an open-topped box with foam into which the rifle can be fitted with a little knife work, or at least a thickly padded slip with a long zip so that the rifle can be lifted out quickly, and also to allow it to be opened up and dried out when (inevitably) it gets damp.

Most of my stalking is for fallow and muntjac in pretty thick woodland. I have had a few unexplained misses, which may have been due to bullet deflection. I use a 7 × 57 with 140-grain bullets. Would I be better to go to a heavier bullet to cut through the brush? Or perhaps change to a bigger calibre?

Transatlantic literature is full of the merits of heavy, round-nosed bullets for use in thick cover, but I think in your case this would be a mistake. The heavier bullet weights for a given calibre tend to be heavily constructed, slow to expand, and are almost certain to go straight through a muntjac without much expansion, making worse problems for you. No matter what bullet weight you use, unless you choose a clear passage for the shot, there will be problems with deflection, not only leading to missing, but worse, to wounding.

On the whole, the combination of 7 mm and 140-grain bullets is an excellent all-round choice for woodland stalking. Even if it means passing up a few chances, be certain of a clear shot before firing.

Boiling out deer heads in the house leads to understandable domestic friction, and even to delay in mealtimes if the cooker is monopolised. What should one do to prepare heads nicely, but avoid starvation and the risk of divorce?

Boiling deer heads do emit a most dreadful smell, so really the process has no place in a normal kitchen. Added to the stalker's irregular hours and the need for large breakfasts at unusual times this could, and sadly does in fact, risk the unfortunate situation you outline.

Stalker R Birt has told me of one neat solution. He visited a car boot sale and bought a second-hand deep fryer for a few pounds. With a suitably rated power extension from the house, trophy preparation can now go ahead quickly and unobtrusively in the garden shed. One caution – make sure that the liner is proof against any chemicals which you add to the water to hasten the process.

Is the use of a bipod unsporting? It seems to iron out some of the skill and uncertainties of stalking, especially on the hill, where most stalkers out for a stag are there for the sport, not just culling. In the latter case I can see that a bipod may be justified.

When scope sights first appeared, fitting one turned your rifle into a 'cad's gun' in some sportsmen's opinions because using open sights involved more skill in getting close to a beast. That has long gone. So too should any lingering prejudice against the use of a bipod where it can help to ensure straighter shooting.

Certainly after a flat crawl a bipod gives a much steadier platform than the usual tottering pile of gunslip, binoculars and the bag with your 'piece' in it. Look at it this way: yes, you are out for fun but also to put effort and skill into spying the hill, selecting a suitable stag, planning the stalk, mastering the vagaries of the wind, choosing the best final approach and

A longer version of the bipod, allowing a steady shot over low cover.

enduring the almost inevitable drenching either from rain or from crawling up a burn. When you do finally arrive at the firing point only one condition applies: the beast must be dispatched as humanely and promptly as you can. This is a matter of ethics and of conscience. Excitement and fatigue make accurate shooting difficult enough without deliberately disregarding what aids modern weapon technology has to offer.

The sport of deer stalking lies with all that goes with a day on the hill, from majestic scenery, the companionship of a professional stalker, many of whom are very good company, a degree of self-knowledge which comes with the experience, and at the end of the day, the satisfaction of having made a clean shot.

I have heard that there is a sort of torch which shows up blood spots when you have lost a deer. Do you know anything about it?

Even with a well-placed heart shot animals may run a long way before collapsing. Lacking the use of a trained deer dog, one is glad for any device which helps to locate a dead or injured beast.

Gerber make the 'Carnivore Blood Tracking Light' which claims to show blood spots clearly as well as serving as a useful LED torch. It costs about £50 from Bushwear (www.bushwear.co.uk). The same firm list 'Blood Revealing Agent' which is a spray. Used after dark in likely places, blood spots react and show up clearly. One stalker I spoke to about this product told me that it really works! There is even a game finder which works like a metal detector, using infra-red technology to detect heat given off by a recently dead deer from 30 yards in cover to several hundred yards in the open.

Even with these devices, there is no excuse for taking dodgy shots.

I have had a bad series of misses and now lack confidence in my shooting. I have tried the rifle and it is spot-on, so what's to do now? I don't usually shoot badly like this.

Most stalkers have suffered this at one time or another, and there are various things which can be checked or done to improve matters.

You have checked your rifle's zero, so that is fine. Otherwise start with the ammo – have you changed batches or mistakenly taken some different loads out stalking? Then check the rifle's zero and if it is off, test the tightness of all screws – scope mounts, recoil stop and tang. If the barrel is free-floating, check that dirt has not accumulated in the fore-end channel. After this, fire some test shots first at the first intersection distance (usually about 30 yards) and then at full range.

With an accurate rifle, there are two likely causes of missing game – over-confidence and flinch. (You should be able to recognise and control plain buck fever.) In the middle of a busy doe cull I have found my success rate suddenly dropping. Maybe one is not holding the rifle properly, hurrying shots or stretching the range more than one should. I solved this by changing to a heavier calibre (in my case a 30-06) just to steady me down and make me hold the rifle correctly. Alternatively, flinching can develop undetected. Many stalkers suffer from it to one degree or another.

This coming autumn I have the chance of some hill stalking for red deer and want to have the right kit. I think I have the clothes, boots and suitable flat hat and would take my normal binoculars (I do quite a bit of woodland stalking) which are 8 × 40. What I want is a telescope, but there seems to be two to choose from: either a traditional long glass, or one of the shorter prismatic ones, with variable power. Which do you suggest?

I was attracted by the technology of the prismatic type of telescope, and tried one of them for two years stalking stags in the Highlands. To be honest, I found the short length quite difficult to hold steady enough for a long session of spying in comparison to the extendible sort, where one could either sit or recline, steadying the scope on a stalking stick driven into the ground at a convenient place for one hand to grip together with the scope and swing as needed from side to side. Admittedly it takes a bit of practice to be comfortable and effective, but the majority of Highland stalkers can't be wrong! Of course one disadvantage is that it can get drowned on extremely wet days while the prismatic ones are more or less waterproof.

You should be able to locate one on the Internet. My battered and museum-worthy glass is 25 ×, with a pull-out tube giving 30 × and 35 × at need. It was made in the Year Dot by Negretti and Zambra but is still perfectly effective. If you can find one made by Greys of Inverness it will be more recent, and they have a very good name.

Incidentally, one essential item you don't mention is a stalking stick. It's best not to rely on borrowing. It needs to be stouter than you need in the woods, and in length to come nearly to your shoulder.

7 The rut and calling

'I s the rut on?' is the question which makes my phone red-hot towards the end of every July, but it's the most difficult to answer. It may be full-on in Dorset while nothing may be stirring in Hampshire. What happens in Inverness is not duplicated in Northumberland. Does can be squeaking madly in one wood but nothing is doing in the next only a mile away. It all depends … On what?

To the woodland stalker, the roe rut is much the same as mayfly time for fly fishermen – very uncertain when it starts, furiously exciting while it lasts (if it happens at all), and over far too quickly! One is fed stories of monster bucks falling over themselves to appear in answer to the merest dog whistle, but in truth it can be a frustrating and disappointing period when all your efforts seem to be doomed to a total blank.

There are always lots of enquiries about the best time, the best calls, the best music to play on whatever whistle you choose, but underlying all this are some basic facts. You are unlikely to call a good buck unless you are in his territory, he does not suspect there is any danger and, most important of all, there must be a doe in season somewhere in the vicinity whose waft of enticing pheromones has come to his sensitive nose.

Yes, they can be totally stupid. A buck came up to my call when I had a large party of the Women's Institute out for a woodland walk. Sometimes, not too often, something will come crashing through the undergrowth (make sure it really is a deer before you look too warlike!) but far more often a buck materialises, just wandering about as if everything was normal – but be quite sure about this: he has heard your squeaks, and knows exactly where they came from. So don't whip up the glasses with white, ungloved hands, or make a grab for the rifle – he will spot you and be gone.

We have a lot to learn from Continental stalkers on the subject, and not only just what squeaks to make and how many of them. One old friend, Udo Geipel, who had fled from the disputed area between Austria and Germany, showed me how to call a buck without making any use of a whistle. He would just choose a tree to stand against to break up his outline, scrape away the twigs to make a bare patch to stand on and then he would just wait – for what seemed ages. Often a buck would magically appear. It took ages before the penny dropped that any rutting buck, hearing something crack a couple of twigs in his territory, would need to investigate. A Polish friend imitated the noise of a buck fraying by agitating the bushes, though I feel that this technique might apply more to woodland red deer. I never did any good with it, anyway!

Is it sporting to call bucks?

On the ethics of calling bucks, one element involved is that there is a degree of skill involved and a great deal of woodcraft if results are to be at all consistent. If you are selective in what you shoot, what difference is there between using a buck's sex drive to gain an advantage and using the fact that a fish is hungry to catch it with a fly or worm?

As a keen photographer, I want to take some pictures of roe in the coming rut and am wondering if it is possible to locate one or more roe rings before the rut, so that I can set up a hide. I imagine they are used year on year in suitable places. How does one go about finding them?

Roe 'rings' are tracks, usually circular or figure-of-eight, made by the deer in July and August. Sometimes, but not invariably, there is a feature – a tree, bush or rock – in the centre. While usually made by a courting pair, rings may also be used by does and fawns, giving rise to the old Scottish term 'spaening rings' in the belief that their use was part of the weaning process.

Not all rutting roe make rings and I will admit that when I have found one it has usually been late in the rut when they were already well worn and obvious, or more often when all activity has just ceased. It's difficult even to predict likely places. I have seen them made in open cornfields, on grassy hillsides, in woodland clearings and in thick cover.

The only record of rings being in use for many years was at Cawdor Castle in Nairn. In his tome *British Deer and their Horns*, JG Millais described several rings there which were so well trodden he and the keepers believed they had been in use for centuries. They were used by a variety of deer of all ages and sexes. He thought there was an element of play in their use, and in this his opinion was shared by 'Snaffle' (*The Roe Deer*). Maybe the settled conditions of a big estate in the nineteenth century contributed to their regular use. His depiction of them, backed up by an artist's keen powers of observation, casts some doubt on the generally accepted view that roe rings are solely an element of rutting behaviour.

One of the curious facts about roe rings is that the deer usually run round them anti-clockwise, which if they are not caught in the act, can be deduced by studying the direction in which the grass or corn has been trodden down. All this shows that roe, like us, have a one-sided bias, similar to being right-handed. Horses, too, have to be schooled out of their preference to lead with one leg rather than the other. If the roe ring develops into a figure-of-eight, then of course, they have to 'change legs' between the two circles.

A close friend of mine was in a high seat in Dorset last night, 2 July, about 9 p.m., when he saw a roe doe with twins. The doe was very recognisable with a split ear. For fun he tried his call and to his amazement the doe responded and came bounding over. She then retreated after several minutes into the nearby wood, only to be chased out by a big mature buck and pursued around the field finally returning to the wood.

Apparently the buck showed all the signs of the rut. Do you think this could be possible or are they just having fun?

The earliest I have called a buck was 4 July, also in very hot weather, and I do think the heatwave we have been enjoying does excite the bucks. It's probably just increased interest rather than serious rutting, or, as you say, they were just having fun.

A roe ring, mostly used by a buck and doe in the rut. There is often an object in the centre, such as a bush or boulder. Rings may take a figure-of-eight form.

Normally there is a good deal of pre-rut activity, possibly part of the process of mate choosing. Once a doe has decided on her consort for the rut, she behaves quite possessively, blatantly egging him on, even while still unwilling to allow mating, and clearly anxious to avoid his straying off. In contrast, bucks seem to pay less attention to defending and remaining in their territory at this time. Maybe one can see a human parallel? Having said that, it is curious that in the later stages of the rut, does appear to welcome the attentions of incoming bucks, which is possibly why calling is more productive then. Being a single-oestrus species with just the one chance of successful pregnancy for the year, this may be something of an insurance in case the primary mating has not produced fertilisation.

Over some years of roe stalking I am confused about the best weather and time of day for calling in the rut. I have always supposed that the best time was from after breakfast to after lunch, and the weather should be warm. There is even supposed to be an advantage in it being thundery, but my diaries show almost random results. Sometimes the weather has been bad but the calling easy and the other way about. Sometimes they come better early in the day, sometimes much later. Is there some other factor which over-rides time and weather? Do they sometimes mate at night, for example?

Calling is both an art and a mystery. The conditions you outline do mostly give the best results. My feeling is that early in the rut a doe is particular about the buck she chooses and there may be a fairly strong bond which prevents the buck from straying off in response to outside attractions, while later on she, and therefore he, may become more promiscuous.

Certainly a good deal of activity, rutting included, does take place at night, especially in periods of full moon. A number of stalkers have told me that calling success during periods of full moon is much reduced. Long ago when I was out on the same ground every day I tracked deer seen against moon phase and demonstrated a good correlation. More moonlight – fewer deer seen at dawn. It stands to reason that if the deer have been hard at it all night, they are likely to be less inclined to move, especially until lunchtime (see page 35).

I will get some stalking during the roe rut in July and hope to do some calling. I've planned to take time off about 20 July for a week. Is this about right, or should it be later?

A lot depends on the weather. Hot and thundery weather can bring the rut on early, but if it's cold you won't see any activity then. One can never depend on it, but normally rutting activity can start about 20 July or so, but the peak of activity is often well into August, say about 7th. Calling tends to be more successful when activity has really hotted up, so if you can, put off your holiday until the end of the month. If your stalking is at a distance and your time reasonably flexible, try to organise some sort of bush telegraph, maybe a friendly local stalker or gamekeeper, to let you know when, or if, the rut has begun.

I have bought a roe call and hope to try it this rut. The instructions are very precise about how many fieps and so on, but it doesn't say what are the best places, or how long to go on trying.

The best places tend to be where you know a suitable buck has his territory and where you can see him coming without either standing in the open like a traffic cop, or where he has to come completely out of cover.

There are three basic noises you can use: first, the squeak of a roe kid, which should bring the mother hopefully followed by the buck. Then there is the similar but lower squeak which a doe emits when she is trying to attract a buck or when one is already in hot pursuit of her. Two-tone calls are used to suggest increasing degrees of urgency and passion. Lastly there is a panic call, loud and high but ending lower, which may indicate a love chase in progress, attracting any other buck nearby.

The most phenomenally effective caller I ever met was a Dr Bertoti from Hungary, whom some older stalkers may remember. He used all three calls in that order, each one repeated ten or twenty times, then an interval of, say, five minutes before repeating it; another interval and he would change to the next type of call, finishing up with the loudest. Then a long wait before moving to another location. Bucks responding may take a considerable time to arrive, so it pays to be patient.

The likeliest period seems to be after breakfast to after lunch, though you will always be meeting stalkers who have had success at other times. You can get a variety of patterns from Bushwear (www.bushwear.co.uk). An audio CD, *Roe Calling with Richard Prior*, is available from the British Deer Society (www.bds.org.uk).

When I am out calling roe, or trying to, I am never clear about standing up (for visibility), sitting down (for camouflage) or sitting in a high seat. Someone told me the last idea won't work, and certainly it hasn't for me!

It isn't any good calling a buck and then not being able to see him! The only time I have needed to sit down is in coppice or similar scrub with a heavily marked browse line so that one needs to be able to see below without moving. Otherwise in woodland it is better to stand to get all-around vision, remembering that a buck may circle to get the wind. Break your silhouette by standing up against a tree, and use gloves and a face mask. In the north where the midges are bad – and being out in early August is asking for misery – anti-midge paste (don't get it in your eyes!), full face veil, bite-proof gloves and trousers tucked into boots are essential. Cammo clothes do help because the buck knows exactly where you are, but minimum movement is the key, so keep your call on a string round your neck so that you don't have to fish in a pocket to give that last encouraging toot!

Some months ago I bought your tape Roe Calling with Richard Prior *and have listened to it time and again, training myself in the art of roe calling. As you may know, it is forbidden to use these calls for hunting in Spain but I am interested in trying myself to check whether I am able to call a buck and at least take a good picture of it.*

I have three different types of call – Hubertus, Buttolo and an Austrian set Faulhaber Rehblatter Garniture *but the translation of the instructions into Spanish is unintelligible. Can you send me some brief instructions?*

Roe calls. Clockwise from right top: Hubertus, Faulhaber Fiep & Kitz, Buttolo. A CD on calling is available from the BDS.

If you start with the fawn call, the doe-in-season call is much the same, but lower in pitch. So if only does respond to your calling, you need to tone the call down (or use another in the case of the Faulhaber set which are fixed). The wooden Hubertus can be adjusted by unscrewing the knob on top. This you can already do. Fine.

With the Buttolo call it is easy to be far too loud, but it works well as a long-range call. You can wrap it in a handkerchief or put it in a pocket. Pressing the bulb produces a doe squeak which is effective if, for example, you see a buck out in a field at some distance. Experiment (preferably not in the woods) by pressing hard on the top of the bulb. If you press firmly enough you will produce an agonising shriek – in German *Geschrei*.

Turning to the Faulhaber set which you have – these are excellent calls. The *Kitz* is obvious. The *Fiep* (you can suck or blow, depending which end you put in your mouth) is the doe-in-season call. With the *Sprengfiep* you hold the knob down to start, and then release it while you are still blowing, producing a noise which they call *pee-eh*. This should be the third in a sequence of calls and should not be used when a buck is very near, or when one is already obviously coming. The *Geschrei* is an agony-call, and can be used to make, for example, a buck which is within shot but behind a bush jump out and give a better chance – but it will only be momentary before he is off. Unless he is completely mad!

One needs to be very patient with calling: blow a set of one type, then wait several minutes before trying the next and so on, from *Fiep* to *Sprengfiep*. Then WAIT. A buck may take two minutes to come – or twenty.

I have been taught that there should be an interval between trying one sort of call (say the fawn squeak) and the next, but watching a rutting buck out in the fields I saw him respond while I was calling, but lose interest when I stopped. Made me wonder if it wouldn't be better to go on until something turns up. What do you think?

Certainly the call-and-wait, call-and wait technique is widely accepted and has called many good bucks, here and on the Continent. The general idea is to start quiet, in case the buck is lying close by, then by degrees call more loudly varying the tone but staying still between each session for several minutes. However, looking back I can remember a number of occasions when a buck has lost interest, as you describe.

It happens that a team of Swedish stalkers has recently been filming the roe rut in England employing the prototype of a new design of call. They were very successful using continuous, rather than spaced calling. However, this was early in the rut and the bucks called were mostly young. A cautious buck might be alerted if, as he approached, your repeated calling failed to be so convincing at shorter range, or was not accompanied by a waft of a doe's pheromones, for example. (They often circle to get the wind.) Curiosity might have brought him in while the caller waited.

It is possible that old stagers might need a more refined technique before they are completely deceived, but there is a lot about calling which remains a mystery.

I have read your books and those of Mr Whitehead but do not find any mention of roe calling using straw. It is very easy to make – you only need a mature rye straw and a sharp knife to cut a reed in the middle of the straw. I learned about this rye call from an old Czech stalker. To use you insert the straw joint (node) into your mouth, press lips round the straw and blow lightly. Is this not known in England?

The technique of using a beech leaf is generally known here, though most stalkers rely on some kind of whistle. The leaf is stretched between the fingers as children do with a blade of grass. A single leaf only lasts for a few calls and so one needs a supply of suitable leaves – preferably handed over the stalker's shoulder, as I have seen it demonstrated, by his attractive attendant.

Many years ago one of my German clients did show me the trick with straw (I think he used wheat) making a slit halfway through the straw about 1 cm long just above a node. The longer the slit (which is your reed) the deeper the note produced. One needs a very sharp, slim knife, craft knife or razor blade and considerable care not to cut yourself. The end you put in your mouth is sealed by the node. The slit faces towards the node and the whole call is about 7 cm (3 inches) long. The whole call goes in your mouth so that the open end just protrudes past your lips. The straw must be really ripe and hard.

Make several, varying the length of the cut and using different diameters of straw.

Blow very gently – you will have made some duds but when one finally sounds off, you will be astonished how easy it is, and what a seductive pipe it makes!

I know there are numerous roe calls used throughout the deer world. Is there any way I can make my own roe call. I know there are options like cherry wood etc.

Unless you are a skilled woodworker, making usable whistle-type calls is difficult to put it mildly. The type with an exposed reed secured with rubber bands is most straightforward but need a good deal of experiment. So far as I know the type of wood used is not important. Lime, because of its lack of grain is favoured by many wood carvers. I have a set which were whittled by hand by an Austrian friend from various hardwoods, using sections of rubber piping to secure the plastic reed. The reed itself needs to be fairly stiff but thin plastic sheet. The thinner, the easier to use. The deeper the hollow, the louder the noise. Tuning these calls is a matter of experiment. When I took up making them myself from blanks machined by a local woodworker, the squeaks as I tried to tune a batch of 50 calls drove my household frantic.

By far the easiest and most effective calls to make use wheat or rye straw, as described earlier.

A collection of hand-made calls. Those to the top right are cut from wheat straw.

I often get barked at when I am out stalking roe in the summer. Can one tell if it is a buck or a doe? Or for that matter, is there any way one can interpret the noise to one's own advantage?

The nearer we get to the rut, the more bucks tend to bark aggressively, and indeed one can take advantage of this display. It is important, however, to know something of the language. Both bucks and does bark, and although one may assume that a gruff tone must be a buck, that is not necessarily the case. Like people, some does have deep voices, and some bucks are rather squeaky!

Most important is to distinguish the alarm bark – a long-drawn *Baaah! Baaah!* often accompanied by stamping, the erection of the white target, and a bouncing run off. Nothing to be done – you have either been spotted or winded. Even then, not all the other deer round about will necessarily take notice of it.

If the bark is the aggressive *Boh! Boh!*, then there is a chance of improving the situation. Stand still, and the beast may show himself as he circles to discover what he has glimpsed or heard, usually circling to get downwind, when all is lost unless your adversary is completely daft or steamed up with the rut. This is a situation where unobtrusive clothing, including gloves and even a face veil, give an advantage, as the buck knows where you are, even if he is uncertain whether you are a rival or an enemy.

The other thing is to reply with as near to a similar bark (but slightly higher in pitch) as you can manage. This takes practice, preferably not in a public place! There is just a chance that a duet will commence, with a thin chance of your seeing him before he sees you. If you are with somebody, there is a great risk of laughing, or being laughed at – but it sometimes works!

Having had a bit of success with calling in the roe rut, how do I go about calling fallow? What calls are available for them?

One has to think about the different habits of fallow deer compared to the roe. Fallow are herding animals, rather than territorial. A major buck establishes a 'stand', where he makes himself obvious, and presumably attractive, to any local does. This he achieves by 'groaning', which has been described as a rhythmic belching grunt, and by spraying the ground and himself with urine and various hormonal additions. Besides the does wandering about, each stand buck is likely to be surrounded by some hopeful immature bucks.

So calling by imitating the squeaks of a doe is inappropriate for fallow, where the females are attracted to the buck, rather than the other way about. Nor is a mature buck likely to stray far off his stand if he hears a distant grunt as if from another buck. Attendant juveniles would, of course, steer clear. All one can hope for by imitating a buck's grunts is to bring a big buck across his stand in defence of it and thereby offer a clear shot. That is, if you have managed to penetrate the usual ring of younger bucks which so often give the game away.

So far as I know there is no manufactured call to help produce this guttural, rather rude noise. Practice is needed, preferably in some deserted place, and with the help of a recording to get the right intonation. There are some good DVDs on fallow, e.g. *The Fallow Deer of the New Forest*, from the British Deer Society shop (www.bds.org.uk/shop).

I know one can call sika stags in the rut, but where can one get the calls?

Yes, sika stags come quite well to the call, and up to now the best source of suitable squeals was the local toyshop. The squeaker in some toys, when extracted (preferably after purchase!) makes the right sound. Eric Masters, at one time the Ranger for Wareham Forest, used to create quite a stir in the shop by going round squeaking all the toys until he found one with the right pitch! Now, thanks to the computer literacy of a stalking friend, we know that calls designed for the American elk (wapiti) can work very well. You can get a set including 'super-attractive cow and calf talking sounds', the 'ACE-2 hands-free bull coaxer' and the 'super-hot ACE-3 hyper cow in heat call' – all with an instructional video – for around seventy dollars. With a little practice, which should be fun for the neighbours, sika whistling can be imitated perfectly.

Try http://www.gunaccessories.com/sceery/DeerElkKitswithVideos.asp

A firm is advertising an electronic deer call. Are such amplifying devices illegal? If they are not, do you think one would be helpful? I have never had much luck with my efforts with a whistle.

When bird protection legislation was passed which made the use of electronically amplified or recorded calls illegal for wildfowlers, deer were understandably not included, and this omission has not since been rectified, so using a recorded call is not outside the law.

Whether such devices would be of real utility to the deer stalker is open to proof when tried against the various whistles etc. which are part of his normal armoury. I can't imagine toting a machine all over the Highlands in case one needed to roar at a stag, though maybe it would work in the forest. Fallow are notoriously indifferent to calling, which leaves sika, roe and muntjac. A prolonged test of hand-held against recorded calls would be quite difficult to stage on an independent basis. So far as the delicate art of calling roe is concerned I feel a machine might need a good deal of practice to operate.

In any case, why do we enjoy venturing out to try and outwit a stag or buck? For fun, or just to fill the larder with rather smelly venison? It's no good saying that any device helps in a duty to reduce numbers – one can only do that by culling hinds and does in the proper season.

Every new device which appears on the sporting scene is greeted with disapproval by the older generation – were not under-and-over shotguns, let alone rifles fitted with scope sights referred to as 'cads' guns'? Possibly the amplified recording will eventually take its proper place, but personally I won't be buying one.

8 Damage and prevention

Damage to crops, trees and garden plants is too often the interface between deer and modern life. Throughout my life as a professional stalker the story has been 'Your deer are eating my trees/strawberries/roses. What are you going to do about it – before the end of the week?'

In fact my original brief on joining the Forestry Commission was to find out why the deer were eating trees faster than the men could plant them – and to stop them doing it!

As against that, the damage deer undoubtedly do has offered endless opportunities to the would-be stalker unable to afford the red-carpet approach of buying time with a guide. Once in, it is up to him to demonstrate to the owner that he is doing a good job and at the same time get on with all the Heads of Department on an estate, such as Head Forester, Head Gamekeeper, Farm Manager and the rest. Doing something positive about damage, however this is achieved, is the high road to keeping and enjoying your stalking.

Usually one is led by the nose to the latest trouble hot spot, which in my experience is always blamed on the deer. A good grounding in definitely identifying the animal responsible is vital at that stage. Spot some wool clumps on the barbed wire and you may get the reluctant answer 'Ah yes, well, the sheep did get in last month!' Cowpats among the trees are a good give-away. Where the maize has been destroyed look for the five-clawed prints of badgers. Insist on walking, not just driving round in the Land Rover listening to a tirade – and not just along the rides but through and across the nettles, bogs or brambles in between. Even before you get to a close inspection of tooth marks or other evidence on the actual damaged plants, it can be surprising what unsuspected rabbit warrens can be disclosed by tramping through the jungle, leading to a red face on the chap responsible for trapping them. I even had one case of severe damage to a collection of prize azaleas which had been blamed on the deer. The new Head Keeper keen to make an impression, had told the beaters 'Come on lads – the pheasants hold in those old bushes, so rattle 'em up proper!' It was beater damage.

In this case I only learned the truth about it by chance years afterwards.

I am getting serious damage to a plantation. I am inclined to blame the deer but can one be sure what is doing the damage, and so take control measures against the right animal?

You don't say whether the damage is to the bark or leaves and twigs. Deer can mutilate trees in three ways: with their teeth (*bark stripping*), with their antlers (*fraying*) and by eating (*browsing*). Other species likely to do damage are hares and rabbits, and voles. If domestic animals break into a plantation they usually leave evidence, such as cowpats or wool tufts.

Bark stripping (apart from that done by park deer) mostly affects conifers at the pole stage, though I have seen bad stripping done by fallow on beech. Long upward scoring will be seen, often with a curl of bark at the top, where the deer has fixed its lower incisors in the bark and jerked its head up. Red and fallow are the likeliest culprits. This type of damage has not been attributed to roe. Sika score the bark with their antlers.

A careful inspection is needed at ground level to identify the correct species responsible for damage. In this case 'deer damage' was caused by rabbits.

Fraying, done either as territory-marking or in the rut, will be at knee-to-shoulder height depending on the deer species. Trees need to be whippy and small enough to fit between the antlers. Roe scrape under the fraying stock; fallow often tousle overhanging branches in their rutting area and again make a scrape below.

Browsing checks and distorts the young tree. The maximum height up to which the twigs are eaten helps to identify the beast responsible: muntjac (because of their habit of rearing up to feed) and roe, up to 1 metre; fallow and sika, 1.6 metres; red, up to 1.8 metres. Deer lack incisors in the top jaw, and so deer-browsed twigs will have a cut-and-tear appearance. Rabbits and hares, on the other hand, bite with a clean diagonal cut. Hares often leave a cut twig lying on the ground below for some reason.

Mice and voles should be suspected if there is a heavy grass mat. Plants are nibbled round the collar at ground level, although bank voles climb and remove small areas of bark which are identified by the minute tooth marks.

The main thing is to go and have a careful look before taking action which otherwise may be wrongly directed and ineffective.

I am a patient man, you have to be to grow trees, but I am fed up with all the guff I'm given about 'deer management'. I have had a chap doing it for years and he gives me a beautiful report every year, but my trees are still eaten. Is all this management stuff better forgotten, and should I look for someone who will just kill the buggers?

I have a lot of sympathy with your problems, and there is no easy answer. The fact is that England is fully stocked with deer. If you create a vacuum, there will be the biblical 'seven other devils' all too glad to barge in from next door and make the last case worse than the first.

Control of damage has to be approached on the lines of a risk assessment. You don't say if you have an arboretum, for example, or if you grow Christmas trees, are trying to establish shelter belts, or have large-scale commercial woodlands. The first two are enterprises where any damage at all is probably unacceptable. No amount of dedicated work by a stalker will stop all damage. He can't be there night and day, but the deer are! Fencing is the only solution.

With shelter belts and also specimen tree planting, tree shelters are usually necessary. Depending on the deer species present, use shelters 1.2 metres high for roe and muntjac; 1.8 metres for fallow and sika, or 2 metres against red deer. Where you need to establish shrubs, short, wide-diameter tubes will get them started even if the tops are eaten off. The root system will get established and some side-growth started. Attention by your stalker should be concentrated in these areas and will help, especially if he weeds out the females in winter.

In commercial forestry, avoid damage by planting wherever possible in comparatively large blocks (deer spend less time at a distance from cover), avoid planting particularly deer-attractive species in places deer tend to favour, and use shelters for any broad-leaved plants. Fraying damage by roebucks can be limited by hard culling of yearling males early in the season; control browsing by ensuring that the population of any deer species is well within the capacity of the habitat to support it. Hungry deer will literally eat anything!

Although shrubs in 400 mm shelter tubes will be eaten, they are establishing a good root system and will bush out later. Timber trees must be protected with the right height of tube.

So your stalker has his place and can help in the situations I mention. I do agree that many stalkers who maybe have a bad conscience try to jolly an owner by producing fancy reports at the year-end which fool nobody. You need to know what he has shot, where he shot it and what he thinks needs to be done next season. A lot of hot air about breathless dawns goes straight in the WPB and does nothing for confidence. Tell him so!

How high can deer jump? I have finally decided to fence my garden in desperation, but don't want to make it more obtrusive than need be. I think the deer that come and eat it are roe, or perhaps fallow?

You should aim at something like 95 per cent protection as a compromise. If deer are just wandering in to feed, 1.8 metres (6 feet) will do the job, but when chased or otherwise frightened, fallow can certainly clear more than this. You must also make sure that they are not provided with a convenient taking-off place (like a tree stump or hump in the ground) just outside.

As important is to understand that deer can both creep under wire, through a drainage ditch for example, and squeeze through remarkably small holes. To deter roe, a mesh size of maximum 10 cm (4 inches) is needed at least in the lower tiers. Otherwise you can clad larger mesh fencing with rabbit netting to do both jobs.

The fence must be complete. The big problem comes with the drive gate, which must also present a complete 1.8 metre high barrier and must not be left open by anybody! It may be worth considering excluding part of your garden from the deer-proof area so that this problem does not arise. Automatic electric gates might be considered.

Making a six-foot fence unobtrusive can be a problem. A partial solution is to erect it close up to a hedge which will soon grow through the meshes, to be trimmed on that side. It could also be concealed by a pergola. The 'big-house' answer to ugly fencing blocking the landscape is, or was, to make a ha-ha, unfortunately a very expensive undertaking. The height for one of these need only be 1.2 to 1.3 metres (4 feet to 4 feet 6 inches) as the deer not only have to jump that high, but get their hind legs up too. It is the difference in deer terms between horse show jumps and the solid obstacles at Badminton!

A traditional ha-ha which does not need to be as high as a conventional fence.

I am driven mad by deer (roe and fallow?) getting into the garden and eating everything – vegetables as well as pansies, and other flowers, and gobbling the rosebuds. It's too complicated to fence – and there is the look of it too, so what can I do?

If total fencing is out of the question, have you thought about deer-proofing bits of the garden? Especially in the vegetable garden one can often put a temporary netting cover or fence round the crop at the critical time. One of my clients loved sorrel soup – but so did the local muntjac! Every time the leaves were

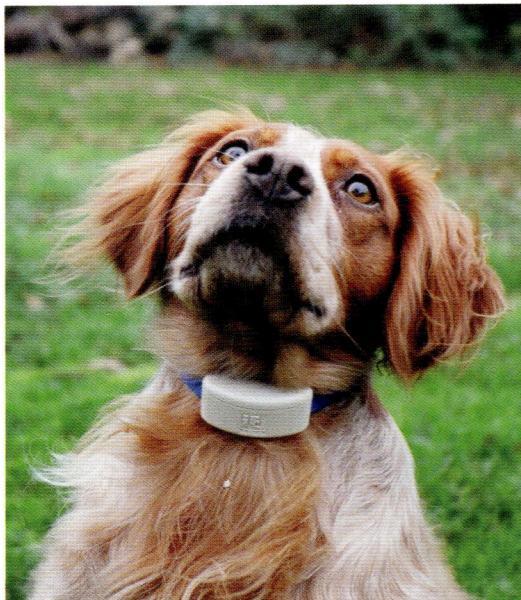

A free-ranging dog limited by an Invisible Fence, and wearing this collar makes an excellent deer deterrent.

big enough the deer were there before the gardener. Luckily the sorrel bed was comparatively small, so a moveable wire netting frame did the trick. Clipped, growing hedges can be unobtrusively fenced by erecting 1-metre high wire netting against the green. The hedge will soon grow through and make the netting totally invisible. If the bottom of a hedge is wired against deer pushing through, they are unlikely to jump at a well-trimmed six-feet high hedge. Existing walls can sometimes be incorporated into a no-go area, but remember to shut the gates!

Deterrents, unfortunately, have a very short-term effect, but spraying roses just as they come into bud with a proprietary deterrent can be effective for long enough to protect the flowers. Some gardeners have had success by putting a cheap portable radio in the critical place and turning it on all night. Neighbours need to be considered. One sufferer locally had the inspiration of making use of old CDs. Hang them up with string and they will glitter in the slightest breeze.

If you have a dog which doesn't mind going out at night, you might consider the Invisible Fence, which in effect trains the dog not to stray beyond a buried aerial. Provided with a kennel for comfort, but with a pop-hole into the garden, he can patrol around from time to time, which is a very good deer deterrent. One warning is not to fix his collar on if there is a risk of a thunder storm. One night unprotected is unlikely to matter once the dog's presence at all times has been established.

Every case is different, but I hope one idea or another will help with this very difficult problem.

My stalking landlord is planting up some game coverts, protecting the trees with shelters. He is very keen, naturally, that they get away quickly. The forestry contractor is putting 1.2-metre shelters on the broadleaves, but only large-diameter tubes like wastepaper baskets on the shrubs. I'm sure the roe will eat them, and we also get a few fallow from time to time, which will browse the tops of the tree species when they come out of the shelters. Am I making a fuss, or is this throwing good money after bad?

No, you are right to make a fuss before the trees are planted, or for sure you will get blamed when the trees are eaten later! The 1.2-metre shelters are fine for roe, but it is necessary to protect vulnerable shoots from passing fallow. If he does not want to use taller tubes now, it will be necessary (if anyone remembers at that stage) that some sort of mesh extension will have to be added, and that will be expensive. So far as the shrubs are concerned, these are vital to give warmth in a game cover, and they need to get away to a good start. However, once they are well established in those wide tubes (they are usually 400 mm long or so) a limited amount of browsing will make them bush out. I say limited advisedly! It isn't just the deer that will have a go. Hares love quickthorn especially, and this is where a continuing effort is essential. On your part this must be to limit the attentions of the deer, and on the keeper's so far as the hares are concerned. If arguments develop about what is responsible, remember that hares bite with a clean diagonal cut, while deer (having no incisors) make a rough bite, or a bite-and-pull to leave a tag of bark hanging.

I live in a village which is infested by roe deer. They eat all the garden plants and get everywhere. It is much worse now because the woods round about aren't stalked any more. Who should I complain to?

Roe soon realise that gardens represent both a sanctuary and a larder bursting with deer goodies. The trouble is that you can't really complain to anyone because as soon as a deer enters your garden, it is nobody's responsibility but your own. It is a good idea to contact the owner of the adjacent wood-land and ask whether they can step up deer control locally. I'm afraid even if they do, the problem is unlikely to go away and you must devise ways of discouraging the deer from raiding. Roe get accustomed to off-putting scents and disregard them after a couple of weeks or so. Don't apply to the zoo for lion dung – it doesn't work any better than old smelly socks (which you can hang up). Flashing lights, of the type found on road works, do have a scaring effect but you must consider your neighbours before trying them. A loose dog dashing about and barking will scare them off, and if the garden is dog-but not deer-proof that should work. The dog needs a pop-hole so that occasional forays can be made at night if he hears someone munching the beans.

My stalking landlord grows a lot of maize and every year he complains about the dreadful damage which the roe and fallow do to his crops.
I am convinced that most of the trouble is badgers, of which we have masses (and TB in the cattle too!) is there any way I can convince him that killing deer won't stop damage done by badgers?

You aren't alone in this problem! It is usually easier to blame the deer, and thus the stalker, for crop damage. Most people in these circumstances don't really want to be convinced of the awkward truth. If your landlord isn't one of those, you could take him round when the soil is a bit moist and show him the tracks of badgers and their hair left on fences. Badgers beat down the stalks to get at the cobs by 'walking up' the plant, but this may also be attributed to deer. The cobs, of course, are eaten somewhat differently because of the badger's formidable dentition, so they will be chomped up leaving punctured toothmarks, whereas deer only have incisors in the lower jaw and flattish molars behind. They have to lever each grain out.

Actual proof can only be obtained by either filming, no easy task as the badger is nocturnal, or by making exclosures to prevent access by deer but not badgers – or the other way round. Expensive and time consuming and in the end unlikely to convince a biased owner.

Long term, building up confidence between owner and stalker by prompt action in other directions where it actually will work may slowly bring him round to accepting that you may know something about wildlife in the country round. That takes time.

The owner of my stalking ground has a lot of Christmas trees. One field has wood-land all round and a buck is creating havoc by fraying. He wants it shot, but it's a beauty and I'd be sorry to do it, pointing out the risk of allowing a horde of yearlings in which would be worse. Can you offer any ideas?

There are certain situations where a degree of damage which would be tolerable in a normal forestry plantation cannot be allowed. Arboreta for one, commercial Christmas trees for another. Really, the only answer is effective fencing and I know you have discussed this without a positive answer.

No matter how we may love them, deer have to fit in with other land uses, just as stalkers have to rub along with their landlords, even when this involves actions which may be repugnant, or likely to be ineffective. Yours is probably such a case.

In your shoes I would shoot the buck having made the case for the likely consequences, as you have done. As a half-way compromise, and slightly to protect your back when further damage does in fact occur, you could offer the idea of electric fencing, using a single white tape (not wire) about 75 cm (30 inches) from the ground. It must follow all dips and bumps, and drains must be gridded or the deer will creep in underneath. Use a fencer with the maximum power permitted and make sure that it is turned on at all times (deer are not like cows and do not, like them, learn to be fence-wise). An effective earth all round the fence is essential. In sandy soils this may dictate running a second (bare) wire below the tape. This is not a full solution, and roe will get in and do damage until you shoot them. As the trees get bigger, one or more high seats will be needed in order to spot the offenders.

Deer are a real nuisance when they get a taste for pheasant feed and start damaging or knocking over feed hoppers. What is the best way to stop the problem?

This is a widespread problem, even to the extent that the roe in some areas are growing notably larger antlers as a result of this supplementary food appearing just when they are growing their antlers! They, and muntjac, ruin spirals and the fallow deer push hoppers over, spilling the contents.

A keeper in Suffolk has kindly sent some details of his method of combating the problem. He finds that four fencing stakes driven in round each hopper holding up large-mesh fencing wire deter the fallow, while a bottom gap less than ten inches high stops muntjac but allows free access for pheasants, protecting them from sparrowhawk attack at the same time.

Alternatively, one can reverse the fence wire so that the largest mesh is at the bottom, leaving no gap. Large-mesh weldmesh bent into a circle is self-sustaining where fallow are not present. It is a matter of experiment to find what works on your own shoot.

The muntjac are devastating my vegetables. They seem to be able to jump or creep over or under any sort of fencing I put up. We are next to a bit of wooded parkland

Fallow in particular demolish pheasant feeding hoppers. A strong weldmesh or woven wire fence allows access to the pheasants and also protects them from raptors.

where I don't think there is any control, or a chance of doing it because of the public. In addition, the badgers make tunnels under the fence which the deer use to get in. What is to be done?

The presence of badgers makes any fencing project short of burying weldmesh to a depth of 30 cm or more ineffective. Nor is there an effective long-term chemical deterrent. You probably have two strategies to consider, depending on your circumstances. One is to cover or fence round individual crops, for example runner beans, with wire netting just while they are vulnerable. It's ugly and time consuming, but the smaller the area enclosed, the more likely it will be to keep the deer out just while it matters.

Alternatively, try electric fencing using a high-intensity fencer unit and white tape. Using a mains unit with an insulated wire to the fence site saves problems with dead batteries. For a start put three tapes at 10 cm, 25 cm and 50 cm from ground level.

The reaction of deer to electric fencers varies, so the suggestion and also the height of the tapes must be subject to trial and experiment. The low wire ought also to deter the badgers, but the herbage along the wire must be kept short, or treated with weedkiller, to avoid shorting. Do not let dogs out in the garden while the fence is live.

My farmer-landlord complains bitterly when he sees deer out on his newly sown crops. I have to admit that one does see quite a few roe and fallow out feeding. Are they actually doing a lot of damage?

One sympathises with a hard-pressed farmer when he sees his crops apparently being eaten off as soon as they grow and it is important to be seen to be sympathetic and actually doing something about it, even if you are unconvinced.

There is a time immediately after germination when cereal crops are attractive to deer, but as soon as the plants start to extend, the nutrient value goes down and roe especially, being browsers not grazers, turn to the newly germinated weed seeds because they are more valuable to them. Close observation (which the farmer is unlikely to do) will make it clear at this stage that the deer's noses are below the level of the crop, searching out the seed leaves of various weeds. Roe deer on the whole are not likely to do

Even when roe are out in the fields, they may be feeding on weed seedlings, not on the crop.

significant damage to ordinary farm crops because they feed on the move and really prefer browsing. The number of deer seen stubbling does give an idea of the density you have allowed. If your ground is also a shoot, any small coverts are precious. Even if there are no young trees for the deer to damage, their habit of creating a browse line when too numerous makes for cold, draughty woods which are less attractive to pheasants. It's your job to understand your owner's other priorities apart from stalking and do your best to collaborate. It's females that reproduce, so up the doe cull. Mature bucks can be left until the proper season.

Even when the crop is actually grazed, experiments on the eventual yield which are detailed in Rory Putman's excellent book *The Natural History of Deer* show that the yield is only very marginally affected. However, nobody ever wins an argument, and if one or two yearling roebucks or fallow prickets have to be sacrificed to keep the peace (and your stalking) they would probably have been part of the cull plan later on anyway.

We have half a dozen roe deer in our garden fairly regularly. We are contemplating planting a new native hedge and thirty or forty garden trees. What protective action should we take to prevent deer from stopping the hedge establishing? We are thinking of planting the hedge with two to three feet high or four to five feet plants – which of these heights would have best survival chance?

The trees we are thinking about are five or six cherry, five or six western red cedar and a mixed variety of twenty or more other species.

For your hedge, I suggest that the solution may be to erect a double fence of wire netting about 1.2 metres high, well pegged down, with a white electric fencing tape on *offset* insulators at 2 feet 6 inches from ground level to deter the deer from jumping in. You may or may not need to run a fencer. Plant two to three foot whips in the middle. Small plants get away more quickly and the roe will not be able to reach them until they have established and bushed out. Eventually your shrubs will grow through the mesh and can be trimmed outside it so that it is invisible while still ensuring that the deer can't creep through in the thornless gaps where you have used broadleaves. Four to five foot plants will soon be above browsing height but will be vulnerable to fraying. They are slower to get away than smaller whips.

If you can't deer-proof the garden (a dog loose at night with a radio collar and buried ring aerial is probably the best), then the ornamental trees will have to be protected. Standards such as cherry need 1.2-metre tree shelters and shrubs like escallonia with wide-diameter plastic mesh tubes. Keep on watering. It won't look pretty at first, but otherwise you will get devastated. Even so, I can't guarantee results.

Offset insulators, preferably carrying white tape not wire, prevent roe from cat-jumping over a fence.

My company has relocated our factory to a woodland site in Hampshire and has plans for landscaping, with amenity plantings of ornamental shrubs and roses. While it sounds very worthwhile, I know there are a number of deer in the area, and seek advice on their likely impact on this sort of planting and whether, once the shrubs are established, there is the possibility of further maintenance expenses. The site is not totally fenced, and the roadways are likely to be in use at least during working hours.

You are perfectly correct in assuming that the local deer will investigate any new planting and continuing damage to vulnerable species is inevitable. To a degree any solution depends on the weight which your company puts on appearance. To do what you outline requires complete fencing to a height of more than 1.8 metres with graded mesh starting at 10 cm for the lower tiers, and with deer-proof access gates automatically operated to open and close with the passage of each vehicle.

Failing this expensive expedient, great care must be taken to choose plant species which are at least less attractive to deer.

Deterrents have no long-term value in preventing deer damage, and electric fencing, in addition to its untidy appearance, is not to be relied on in these circumstances.

Probably the most practical solution would be to protect individual standard trees with plastic tubes (tree shelters) until well grown. A height of 1.2 metres is enough for roe, but 1.8 metres is needed where fallow deer are involved. Ground cover has to be unprotected, and choice depends on the soil type. Shallon, for example, is mostly untouched and some types of berberis. A good reference is Coles *Gardens and Deer – A Guide to Damage Limitation* (Swan Hill Press, 1997) or my own *Trees and Deer* (Swan Hill Press, 1994).

How soon can I take tree shelters off? I hate to see a callus developing where the plant rubs against the tube to make a weak place. In addition some hardwoods, beech in particular, do not seem to like growing in a shelter and the sooner it can be taken off the better. I use 1.2-metre tubes as we don't have fallow round here.

In commercial or large-scale planting, the main function of a tree shelter is to prevent the plants from being browsed, checking their growth, spoiling their shape and increasing establishment costs from beating-up and a longer period of weeding. Unless you have very particular trees which have also to be protected from fraying, it is probable that the sacrifice of a few stems round the outside where a buck marks his territory will be more than balanced by fairly early removal of the tubes once the trees have made enough growth above the shelter and are safe from browsing.

Once the trees are unprotected, if possible reduce the weeding, especially in the rows rather than between them. This will prevent the deer getting access, and incidentally offering some alternative browse. A low growth of bramble can make a good prickly barrier. It is advisable to keep a careful eye on any yearling bucks in the area as they can do considerable fraying damage and need to be kept to reasonable numbers. A mature buck left in place should look after this, but the stalker may have to give him a hand if the plantation seems to attract young bucks. Needless to say, deer control is made much easier if the rides are planned with wide areas or with clearings where a high seat can command the vulnerable trees until they are out of trouble.

9 Conservation and management

The word 'conservation' is too often taken to mean preservation. Far from it – the proper definition is '*the wise use of a renewable resource*'. The so-called Balance of Nature is a pipe dream. Nature is changing all the time, and not necessarily the way we would like. You only have to look at the problems in some American National Parks which were founded on the principle of letting Nature have its way to see the disasters that built up over the years. In the end active management had to replace the original concept of non-intervention and in some cases drastic action had to be taken to preserve the very thing that was meant to be saved. One instance was the necessary cull in the Yellowstone Park of fifteen thousand elk, just to preserve the habitat which the population had outgrown. There are those enthusiasts who think that a balance can be restored in our own country by reintroducing natural predators. Wolves and lynx have been proposed. The latter was the subject of an experiment in Europe which has shown that on average a lynx kills one and a half roe deer per week. Supposing our roe deer population is half a million (it is probably more) the necessary annual cull just to keep numbers stable is 30 per cent or one hundred and fifty thousand. Even if we liberated one thousand lynx they would only eat half that number of roe, without considering the other five deer species which live in Britain, all of which are also in need of control.

Doubtless wolves are more devastating predators than the lynx. However, the promoters of their value released into the countryside as a natural population control might have something of a public relations problem. It is a myth, though, that they eat people – very often anyway. Being sensible animals, rather than feasting on elusive wild deer (or children) they would go for the easiest prey, such as our domestic sheep and pigs, not to speak of their favourites (as I was told in Portugal): ponies and donkeys. At a recent scientific conference it also emerged that introduction of the grey wolf to Scotland could bring with it no fewer than eleven pathogens offering a disease risk to native animals and humans.

Nobody wants to see deer starving because there are too many of them. They also have to fit in with life in an overpopulated and over-used island. Even the specialist conservation bodies, many of which shrink from the notion of killing anything, have woken up to the need for control because the deer are numerous enough to conflict with their own particular, often narrow, interests. This may lead to over-reaction and disregard of the fact that deer are large and beautiful animals needing some of the humanity we extend unthinkingly to our cats and dogs, and capable *with management* of producing significant cash flow and employment possibilities.

Extremism is to be avoided at all costs. At a meeting of senior conservationists discussing the restoration by natural regeneration of the ancient Caledonian Forest, the local man stated that all the deer in that part of Scotland would have to be eliminated.

'What about the people who live and work in the glen?'

'They can go elsewhere!'

'And how long would this clearance need to go on?'

'Oh! About three hundred and fifty years.' And he seemed to be in earnest about it.

'And who would pay?' To this he had no answer.

The aims of management

What really are the aims of deer management? No serious business can possibly run these days without a 'Mission Statement' or words to that effect, but what can we poor stalkers do in order to give direction to what we are trying to do? Ask the landowner to tell you what he wants you to do and you will probably get the answer 'Go and talk to the Head Forester, the Head Keeper and the Farm Manager and stop them bellyaching, but don't shoot the deer which my wife can see from her bedroom window – and remember that we want to keep some bucks for the foreigners who are coming in August!' The Head Forester will probably want you to kill the lot, the Farm Manager doesn't want wheel tracks on his crops, but does hope you won't let that party of fallow appear before harvest is over, while the Head Keeper is letting sixty days' shooting this year and can't do with you disturbing his birds until the end of January. I am exaggerating, but you know what I mean.

A formidable management problem arose in a park herd of mainly dark fallow where the annual cull had to include at least fifty fallow does, '*But don't shoot Jane!*' Jane was a dark fallow doe indistinguishable from her fellows, but who came up to the dining room window each morning for the breakfast crumbs. It is to the enormous credit of three successive stalkers that she was eventually found dead of old age. Or just luck? We all need it.

Management in our terms means attempting to fit a reasonable population of healthy deer into the mass of conflicting interests of an over-used island. This has to involve quite a bit of give-and-take on the part of those closely concerned. Sometimes the deer have to give way for overriding reasons – arboreta, intensive production of Christmas trees and some horticultural crops for example. In other circumstances, say large-scale forestry and arable or mixed farming land they can have a place and even contribute a modest cash flow. The prime job of the deer manager is to listen carefully before deciding on the proper balance. I learned that lesson early in my career as a deer manager when I was accused by my Forester boss of 'running a private zoo at his expense'. Don't fall into that trap! We should try to convince all concerned that we have their best interests at heart.

My stalking doesn't have much woodland, just one sizeable wood, but quite a few roe spill out along the hedges all summer. Are these likely to be mostly yearlings? Because of the crops it often isn't too easy to see exactly what they are. Should I cull them heavily as non-territorial juveniles?

It is true that yearlings tend to wander along hedgerows when they are thrown out of their parents' territories in spring, and if undisturbed there, can hang about until harvest. Basically it's a good idea to take what you can of the yearling buck cull from within established territories, as these individuals have not shown enough spirit to attract the attentions of the resident buck, and are likely in consequence to be poorer specimens than those ejected and colonising the hedges. Having said that, hedgerow deer are very visible and should be thinned as a contribution to good relations with those concerned more with farming and forestry.

Do not assume that they are all yearlings. Occasionally an old buck losing his territorial drive will decide to take up residence in a quiet hedge or planted-up corner. Some of these have poor, going-back heads, but sometimes one can find a cracker!

The muntjac are being endless trouble in my coverts, especially by putting up the birds in droves on big days and the stalker just doesn't shoot enough to control them. I'm going to tell the keeper to shoot them regardless. Must I get him a rifle, or will the shotgun in his very experienced hands do the job? I will buy him some BBs to keep in the Land Rover.

I wonder if your stalker is doing a good job otherwise, as fallow are potentially more damaging and you have plenty in your area. He isn't going to be very happy if you do as you suggest. Apart from that, muntjac are covered by the Deer Act, and so you can't use a shotgun. If it can be shown that they are doing damage, and this is to growing crops or any other form of property and other methods of control are not possible, then your keeper could, with your written permission, use a shotgun, but only with AAA shot, nothing else. Whether covert shooting could be regarded as property in this context has not been established.

Have you thought of making the stalker's time more productive by offering to widen some of the rides? It's worth talking it over with him, rather than antagonise a useful ally.

I stalk on some land which is also a pheasant shoot, let to a syndicate. The owner is anxious that I keep the deer down but I can't get on with the cull because the keeper says that stalking disturbs his birds. Does stalking really worry pheasants – the keeper is about all the time anyway – and have you any advice about satisfying my landlord without getting all wrong with the shoot?

This is a perennial problem up and down the country and has more to do with managing people than deer! I would say in answer to your first question that provided you keep away from release pens in the evening (which may put the birds off roost) and avoid stalking on shoot days and one day beforehand, then you are unlikely to conflict with the interests of the shoot. Obviously there are exceptions to this, for instance if the keeper relies on dogging in to stop his birds straying and you happen to stalk up a critical hedgerow the wrong way.

Game shooting is more important financially than stalking, so it's up to you to prove that you understand and go along with the keeper's worries and discuss any problems with him until he and you form a team, not enemies. After Christmas the pressure on most shoots tends to ease, and by that time he may be agreeable to you doing more for the doe cull. After all, deer spoil many drives, either by eating the undergrowth which holds birds or charging across a flushing area at the critical moment, so he doesn't want too many either. If this means that you still really can't shoot as many deer as your owner wants, then it's a good idea to explain the situation to him, telling him at the same time the steps you have already taken to get along with the shoot. He may then talk to the shoot tenant direct to arrive at a compromise, but it's better by far to try hard to work together.

I seem to be getting in more and more difficulty with my roebuck cull. I try to follow all the experts' advice and leave my trophy bucks until they are in good summer coat, but my stalking is mostly thick woodland with mostly hazel and bracken underneath and arable fields between. Although the roe are out in the fields in spring, the bigger bucks have disappeared early on, and even the yearlings vanish as soon as the crops are sprayed or grow up a bit. Then I see practically nothing until the harvest is off. Should I try to get my yearlings in March, and then get on with the mature bucks? I have quite a big cull and it just isn't getting done. Advice please.

The old idea was to start the buck season on 1 May, and indeed that is what I used to do in my professional days. However, things are not the same now, most likely due to climate warming as well as changes in the farming scene. The leaf comes earlier in the woods, and fields are sprayed repeatedly which discourages the deer from feeding there. Under your circumstances you have to make a start earlier, but always within the law. In consequence you may not shoot yearling bucks in March, but there is every reason to get going in April in the southern counties at least. Mature bucks will be occupying their territories long before they are in summer coat, and while something of the pleasure of the buck season is lost in taking bucks which still look scruffy with the remains of their winter coat, your obligations to the landowner to protect his crops may dictate this policy. You cannot depend on getting many bucks in the rut if your ground is as thick with bracken as you describe.

Yearlings can be picked off in the fields while they are still there, and you will have another opportunity to complete your cull after harvest when there are often a number of roe out on the stubbles.

I am a tenant farmer with a small dairy herd and some arable. My landlord has let the deer stalking and the tenants only shoot the bucks, so my farm is over-run with deer which are eating all my spring bite and later they lie in the corn, starting it lodging. I've complained, but they don't do anything. I know deer are wild animals, but surely I must have some sort of redress as I'm not allowed to shoot the marauders. Can you help?

One has a lot of sympathy with your predicament, which is not unknown where stalking tenants take a short-term view of deer management, only bothering with the big bucks. We all know that this leads to overpopulation and loss of quality, but the word doesn't spread as it should.

You do have redress. The bible for this is a book called *Deer: Law and Liabilities* by Parkes and Thornley (Swan Hill Press, 2nd Edition 2008). They state:

> In England and Wales the law does not confer on the Occupier the right to take deer in this situation unless by agreement with the landowner or the person holding the shooting rights to the deer. In circumstances where the tenant of an agricultural holding suffers crop damage from deer and is restricted from culling them – i.e. the rights are vested in the owner or someone else and no written permission

exists – a claim for compensation can be made under the Agricultural Holdings Act 1986.

To claim compensation, a tenant must give his landlord written notice within one month of the damage becoming evident and give him the opportunity to make an inspection of a growing crop before it is harvested or, if damaged after harvest, before it is removed from the land. A written notice of the claim is then sent to the landlord within one month after the expiry of the year in respect of which the claim is made. For the purposes of such a claim, a year normally ends on 29 September or another date agreed with the landlord. Where the shooting rights are held by a third person (e.g. a shooting tenant or syndicate), the landlord is entitled to be indemnified by the third party against such claims, which may be settled by arbitration under the Act.

I have been told that one should not shoot trophy roebucks until after the rut, so that they could pass on their good genes to their offspring. In the sort of woods that I stalk, if I don't get what I want in April and early May, or in the rut by calling, there isn't much chance of seeing them at all, let alone getting a shot. What ought I to be doing to get it right?

Obviously you are careful about your roe management, and want to do the best for them. In places where there is something of a free-for-all, with promiscuous shooting of practically anything legal and male, rules have to be made to ensure survival of the species.

In your case I expect you are making a spring census, and from this, constructing a shooting plan divided into age classes. The textbook suggestion is 60 per cent of the buck cull should consist of yearlings, 20 per cent middle-aged and 20 per cent old. To maintain numbers the cull of does should slightly exceed the total of bucks shot. To reduce the herd, more does should be culled. Sticking to this, a proportion of your most promising young bucks should be surviving until they are at least five or six years of age. By this time they will already have successfully held a territory for three or more years, competing for and serving at least one doe each season and thus passing on their characteristics even if your shooting plan takes them early in their last year. Nothing is worse than not shooting enough (especially females of course) and allowing a large and unbalanced population to develop.

It has been observed that while a doe may be very particular about the buck she accepts for the first service each rut, she may then appear to be much more promiscuous. We have no way of knowing which buck will prove to be the sire of next year's kid or kids resulting from multiple matings. In a species with only one oestrus per year, this may be an additional insurance against infertility.

With the doe season soon on us, I am doubtful about shooting does while their kids are still with them. Don't they learn a lot from their mothers, even though they are weaned? Even on that point, we do find some roe does still in milk in November when I go north for the doe cull. What should be the guidelines?

You make two valid points: roe kids do learn from their seniors through their first winter, and indeed some do continue to suckle much later in Scotland than in southern England. So far as suggesting some guidelines for you, this depends on the scale of the roe population and the cull you have to achieve. If the density of all species of deer is high, then one of the most important functions of the doe cull is to ensure that there is enough food left to see the breeding stock through winter and spring. If through understandable reluctance to make orphans you fail to shoot enough, the young are the first to suffer and the whole community loses quality while damage to crops and forestry increases for lack of natural food. If you only have a few does to get and plenty of time to do it, then you can be more overtly humane in your selection of does to shoot. It is a bad policy to leave culling until February because of the extra food consumed by animals which should have been taken earlier. Also the weather can get bad and completing the cull is impossible.

On hill land in the north where heavy snowfall is to be expected, the reproductive rate is likely to be lower than on low ground so a smaller percentage need be shot, and maternal help is more important to get kids through the winter. Unless under pressure of large numbers, the stalker under these circumstances can concentrate on taking kids until the New Year, especially one of a pair of twins, to give the survivor a better chance.

The books all tell one what proportion of the deer herd one ought to shoot and what percentage of each age class.

I am going to try and make a count of the roe deer on my stalking this spring but in my thick woodland somehow doubt that what I see is anything like what I've got. Have you got any advice on how to go about it, and what margins of error are likely?

Sad to say, it's easier to lay down the law about deer management on paper than carry theory into practice in the field! All the books can do is to lay down some guidelines which you have to interpret according to the conditions you encounter on your own ground.

Useful questions: What numbers have been shot in past seasons?
Are there more or fewer now than in the past?
Are the deer in good condition?
Are there too many on the ground?
What is the sex ratio?
Is there much forest or crop damage?
Are the roe competing with other deer species?

As you see, there is a lot to think about without trying to make a physical count.

If you have had the stalking for a few seasons, or there are reliable past records, this gives a base. Condition can be assessed from body weight and obvious thinness. Don't go too much on their looking scruffy – this is normal as the winter hair is shed in spring before the new coat comes through.

Having too many deer is bad for landlord relations as well as for the deer themselves. Towards the end of winter study the browse line. Are the woods noticeably clearer below one metre than above? Where ivy grows on the trees, there will hardly be a leaf left to this level if the deer are pressed for food.

By all means go out early and late to see what is to be seen and take notes – separating the sexes and noting mature and young bucks separately. It's rare to find equality between sexes, which is ideal, but more than one and a half females to each male indicates that last year's doe cull was insufficient.

Good relations with other land users are vital: listen for complaints of damage – and go and check them. Look out for intensive areas of damage. Scattered damage is usually not so important except for special situations – arboreta, cricket bat willow plants, and of course gardens.

Large deer species compete with roe and muntjac. Fallow, red and sika deer can reach up higher and can completely deny their food sources to the smaller species.

The actual numbers that any place can support depends on the habitat. I feel that the impact of deer on their environment is a good guide for the practical deer manager to back up his theory, important though that may be.

I hear that a research project has been started to find out about deer killed by cars. As there seem to be masses everywhere, what is the point? Convince me and I'll tell you about them round here.

The Deer Initiative launched research into road accidents involving deer.

This is something which in other countries is taken very seriously indeed, but up to now we have had no hard facts because nobody has the duty of recording them.

Figures are available for the three years, January 2003 to December 2005; the results from this research produced details of deer-related road accidents involving thirty-one thousand deer and five hundred human injuries with several fatalities. Damage to vehicles is estimated at more than eleven million pounds annually. The work continues.

Even from some small-scale studies, the number of deer killed in traffic accidents is very high – high enough in some hot spots to make nonsense of deer management plans in the vicinity. If, say, 10 per cent of your potential annual increase is being wiped out it's no good making meticulous cull plans based on theoretical production figures. If a dozen of your best bucks lie squashed on the road, inviting paying guests to come and stalk them is pointless. However important this may be, other considerations have a wider significance.

Deer are large creatures and can do extensive damage to vehicles, and cause injury or death to driver and passengers. In stark terms each incident can involve heavy personal and public costs and extra strain on the emergency services.

Without good data on where these accidents are liable to happen and the extent of the problem, no action can be expected from the authorities. The design of roads, the landscaping of verges and embankments and the treatment of adjacent woodland all need to be taken seriously by architects and civil engineers, many of whom have cost as a prime concern and would only be swayed by well-researched data. Do I need to mention the agony inflicted on the many which are not killed outright? That is another thought which I hope will induce everyone to collaborate.

You may obtain more information from www.deercollisions.co.uk

There has been a suggestion recently to abolish the close season for stags. Could you tell me what your feelings are about this, and what justification there is for having a close season for males, or not?

From a humanitarian point of view, it doesn't matter to the stag whether he is shot at one time of year or another, so why should we bother? The reasons are fundamental to the management of deer in this country, not only in maintaining a healthy population in balance with its environment, which is one of the primary aims of the deer manager, but in reducing the damage suffered to their crops by farmers, foresters and gardeners.

The reason is, sadly, human frailty. No matter what attitudes or high-flown theories are bandied about, the bare truth is that when someone with a rifle has some deer in front of him, he will prefer to shoot a male. One has only to look at our herds of fallow deer to see a vast preponderance of females which is the direct result. British fallow trophies have little or no international value, so commercial exploitation has nothing to do with it. Quite the reverse. If they had, more trouble would be taken to preserve the best males.

Deer are not monogamous, so not matter how few males are left, virtually all breeding females will be pregnant. If, instead of 50 per cent females, which is desirable, 70 or 80 per cent of the total herd are female, their reproductive rate will be vastly increased, and thus the problems of over-population and under-culling multiply. This applies to all species. Nobody can dispute that shooting females when they are heavily pregnant or with dependent young is highly undesirable. So the main purpose of restricting the times when male deer can be shot is to channel the efforts of stalkers into the often hard and unsavoury task of culling sufficient females within their open season.

My bit of roe stalking is in Northumberland, and consists of mixed woodland and fields. The roe seem to be healthy but the heads they grow are rather poor. Should I weed out the worst, or can I put out salt or feed of some sort to improve the antler growth?

The basic reason for a roebuck putting out poor antlers is lack of rich food, principally protein, during the winter when they are growing them. That is far more important than any efforts one can make in selective shooting. It is unlikely that salt will help – roe are usually reluctant to take to it. Sometimes they do acquire the habit of visiting high-protein supplements, either liquid or solid, put out for cattle or sheep, and I have seen some spectacular heads which were grown as a result. Putting them out specially for the deer is a chancy idea considering the expense, but you might visit one or two farmers round about to see if deer are visiting theirs, and if so, what type they favour.

Probably a better investment of time and money would be to improve the winter browse available to the deer. If it is your own land, or in collaboration with the owner, you might consider widening any tracks so that scrub grows along the edges, or making holes in the canopy by careful thinning to let the sun in for the same purpose. If you are on low ground you may be lucky enough to have bramble, and maybe ivy grows up some of the trees. Both of these are sought-after browse. Otherwise a few goat willow plants, protected in their early years and then pruned low, will be appreciated.

Of course you need to make sure the herd is not excessive, and this can most easily be assessed by how hard any growth is eaten off by mid-winter. There is only one way to do that – shoot more does progressively year by year until the browse line becomes less well defined. You may be surprised how big a cull is needed to make any difference!

I have stalked roe for years on a patch of ground in Wiltshire. We now start to see muntjac which personally I don't welcome. How can I eliminate them?

The spread of muntjac seems to be inexorable and I don't think your attempt at a Canute act is likely to succeed. There are some steps which you can take to favour the roe and limit muntjac numbers to some extent, but the success of one species or the other depends a lot on the habitat. The first rule must be to shoot muntjac on sight, even if you are out for a roe, or even in the middle of a stalk for one.

If your woods are thick, the muntjac will be difficult to see and from their habit of skulking about without really stopping they are tricky to shoot. Roe are also more to be seen in the fields than they are. Hopefully there are some rides in the woods which can be used or modified to make a few high seats worthwhile. Muntjac can be encouraged to show themselves by judicious baiting. Various feeds have been suggested, such as fruit, nuts, or a slowly leaking fruit juice carton placed on a tree stump.

Although your principal interest is the roe, now that you have another species it will be helpful to study them, both on the spot and by reading. We now have a primer on the subject: Charles Smith-Jones' *Muntjac – Managing an Alien Species* (Coch-Y-Bonddu Books). In the end you may find yourself interested, even fascinated, by these enigmatic foreigners and eventually join the growing band of enthusiasts.

I'm in a dilemma – according to the rules we try to get 60 per cent of our cull as yearling bucks, and as usual haven't managed to get enough. With the fields cleared there are quite a few to be seen on the stubbles, but they all look good to me. Is it better to get the number and risk shooting some promising animals, or finish up short and hope for better things next season?

There are two important things to remember – the antlers yearlings grow do not necessarily indicate what they are going to show later. Possession of a territory and therefore a better standard of life in later years can turn a poor-antlered yearling into a Gold medal. Studies with marked deer make this fact, not surmise. Again, if you leave too many strong yearlings, your major bucks will certainly turf them off the place next spring!

Remember that if one makes a mistake and shoots a potentially good yearling, only a year is lost. Make the same sort of mistake with a middle-aged buck and it will take four or five years to replace him.

In areas where the winters are hard or the feed short there is often a marked difference in size or condition between yearlings, even between siblings, and in that case one can be quite selective in culling that age class. In better districts the breeding success and survival are higher, the majority are big and healthy and the deer manager has to harden his heart and go for the number which is thought best for the well-being of the deer and the way they fit into other land uses.

We have a block of blanket-planted conifers which is infested with roe and some reds. It's almost impossible to get on terms with them, so we are widening the rides.

What are the best bushes or whatever to plant along the ride-sides to attract them out?

You don't have to widen all the rides, just make wider bits about one hundred yards long and six to eight yards on either side of the track. A block between makes the approach more feasible. Try not to open the end of rides to let in cold winds and encourage unwelcome visitors. Where the ground suits, you can erect a high seat to overlook the clearing, preferably with an approach path from another ride.

You don't say how far up the hill you are, but on this sort of ground willow is the best bet. Once established it can be coppiced periodically to produce new growth for the deer. Choice of species depends on elevation: osiers on low ground, higher up goat willow and grey sallow are likely to grow except in very exposed, high locations, where eared willow may be the only choice. Once planted out either use a tree shelter or lay a thick layer of brush on top and let it grow through.

Take cuttings in March and root them in a nursery before planting out with protection until they are growing strongly. More exotic species are attractive to deer and may be obtainable from nurseries at the end of the season as rejects. Strong regrowth is what is needed.

The ground around here is a mix of 35 per cent grass farm, 35 per cent crop and the remainder a mix of rough ground and woods. The ground that I have has two small woods, one about three acres and the other only one. However it is surrounded by large forests. In the two woods there is a constant supply of roe passing through. So far this year I have taken one yearling, three two-year-olds and one mature, making five bucks. The only reason that I took two of the two-

Pre-rooted willow cuttings can be used as ride-side deer attractors for browsing and fraying.

year-olds was because they were injured, probably by vehicle accidents. There are two resident family groups in the woods and they have been there for some years now. These groups consist of five and three does with anything from two to four bucks at any time. The question is how many does and bucks do I cull?

It is always difficult when you are both a corridor and have probably quite attractive cover too, what there is of it. As you have noticed, even when you have what amounts to stable resident groups of roe, their make-up varies from week to week. I suspect that you might hold a couple of territory-holding bucks in the summer with a shifting population of younger animals. By rule of thumb you ought to shoot more does than bucks, so for this winter try for six or seven does. If the cover in your woods is heavily browsed, or neighbouring farmers complain, maybe one or two more. You have to feel your way. Then next spring look carefully to note the buck to doe ratio and also how many kids per doe have survived.

With forestry next door you will be on the receiving end of yearling emigration, and next summer's buck cull ought to consist mainly of this age class, if possible leaving the two to three-year class and rewarding yourself with possibly one mature buck. Something like that. It's a combination of guesswork and doing more looking than shooting to get a feel of the trend.

The country round here is hotching with muntjac and all the gamekeepers are complaining of what they do, eating from the hoppers and flushing birds at the wrong moment. I enjoy stalking them and am welcome on several places, but I don't like shooting does. Either they are pregnant or in milk – apparently always one or the other, so I prefer to let them go, shooting all the bucks I can. I've been criticised for this, but what can one do, still behaving humanely?

This is a horrid dilemma for any muntjac stalker. They are non-seasonal breeders, having young at any time of year, and they mate again very soon after parturition. Shooting pregnant does is repugnant, though it is the only way to be sure of not leaving an orphan. However, one has to face the fact that the muntjac population is out of hand over large parts of this country and unless the stalking fraternity make a desperate effort to get on top of numbers, one day draconian culling measures will suddenly be imposed involving wholesale and unpleasant methods. One has only to look at the darker parts of New Zealand's red deer past to realise what can happen when an imported species gets out of hand. So my advice to you is – harden your heart and shoot muntjac does as opportunity offers. That is the only way to reduce the breeding population. Yes, some fawns will die, but Nature always looks to the future of the species, not the individual, and in the situation you find yourself, distasteful as it may be, you should go ahead.

Now that we are allowed to take buck fawns either before or after the mother is culled, can you suggest whether we are morally right to shoot male fawns in the winter and what chances they have of survival if they are left to survive as best they can?

Under the Regulatory Reform (Deer) (England & Wales) Order 2007 a dependent male fawn or calf may be killed if they are about to be, or have been, deprived of their mother. In the easy conditions over southern England a roe fawn orphaned after Christmas will probably manage pretty well, although its general health and therefore the antlers it grows through life may be affected. The same probably applies to the early months of the doe season unless we get the promised severe winter. Farther north, climate and habitat may reduce those chances to the point where it is a kindness to shoot it at the same time as its dam.

The morality of shooting these buck fawns, or the advisability from a deer management point of view, depends on population density. Where a stalker is under such light pressure that he can afford to pick and choose, one can be selective, shooting poor fawns out of pairs of twins regardless of sex, and taking adult does which have not bred, or with one or more poorish fawns. Where he has a big cull to achieve, his success in reducing numbers will possibly affect the amount of feed available to the survivors later in the winter. In these circumstances I would take the doe first and hope for a few seconds to take the followers at the time, or come back the next morning, when they are likely to be hanging about.

I have just taken on a bit of wettish farmland in Caithness and there seem to be three families of roe on it: three does with twins and three bucks. The farmer seems to be relaxed about them. What cull plan should I follow to keep matters stable? The farm is surrounded by bogs and scrub where there are plenty of roe, so we may get some incomers too, but I want to do it carefully.

On the population you have seen, all that needs to be done this winter is to shoot one doe. The owner may like a bit of venison as well as knowing you are active in his interests. If your three does have twins, they are doing well. Then I would suggest you see what happens next spring. You may well find that more roe appear from round about, and by April I expect there will be some yearling bucks trying to find a home and you could take a number of them, leaving your resident mature bucks to keep the peace. Much depends on what goes on on the neighbouring ground. If the stalker there is hard on his deer, you may get fewer yearlings but a few mature bucks displaced by disturbance. Otherwise you may get a substantial spill-over of surplus young deer. When you have got to know the place better, I would suggest you fix your cull on the general basis of more does than bucks and more yearlings than mature bucks. In this way the resident population should be stable and you take your cull largely from the incomers. Under your circumstances it is impossible to lay down a rigid cull plan when every-thing depends on immigration.

I want to build up the roe in my woods within reason, but we already have fallow in some numbers. Can the two co-exist, or is there too much competition for the roe to succeed? We mostly have small pheasant coverts, mixed conifer and hardwoods, with one block of seventy acres in farmland.

Speaking generally, roe like denser undergrowth while fallow favour woods where the closing canopy has thinned any understorey. The two species can live together, and do in many places, especially in more extensive stretches of woodland. Where there are fallow rutting stands, roe tend to say clear of them from September to November but may find temporary lodging in smaller coverts and hedgerows.

In your case if you have many fallow they will eat out the woods, which will be bad both for pheasants and roe. If you already have this problem, it's the first one to tackle, and the only way to do it is to shoot does – hard.

The other consideration is habitat. On so many shoots small coverts were planted some years back, often with difficulty to get the trees to grow, but once in place and holding birds, essential management tends to get forgotten until suddenly it is noticed that those drives don't work as well as they once did. Work to re-establish the shrub layer will benefit the shoot and the roe.

We lost a lot of sika and roe fawns in the silage-cutting this year. The contractor's men drive such huge machines at such a rate that they couldn't possibly know what is going underneath. Is there anything one can do to avoid this dreadful slaughter?

It is a disaster when silage or hay-cutting coincides with the peak of fawning. The mutilation and heedless killing of young deer is horrific and also, on a very practical level, if the remains are baled up, each bale is foul and wasted.

Some years ago Laurent Perrier ran a competition for the best method of preventing the problem. Finding a solution was fraught with difficulties, mainly because nobody is going to carry out a critical farm operation at half-speed, and as you say, the size and speed of modern machinery compound the difficulty. For this reason, no attachment to the tractor is practicable. Other ideas are time consuming and not necessarily effective, such as dogging the field the previous evening. The dog may not scent close-lying fawns, or the mothers may take their fawns back again during the night.

The competition was won by trials of small blinking traffic lights such as are set round holes in the road, put at intervals round the field. This needs somebody on the spot who cares enough to spend time and money, acting in concert with farm staff.

How ought I to organise my roe shooting plan for the year? It's all right talking theory, but I can only stalk odd weekends through the year and there just isn't the time to try to do a census or whatever. There are a lot of walkers on my patch and I can't get at the does before the end of the shooting season, though I did manage to get eight in February, which seems to have thinned them out noticeably. Advice please for very much a part-timer.

I should think that half the stalkers in the south suffer as you do! At least you have given me a clue with the size of your doe cull. If you think that's enough, then in typical pheasant-shooting country you can probably take three mature bucks and five yearlings. Take the yearlings early if you can, and if you feel through the summer they are being replaced by incomers, then you can safely take a few more when you see what come out on the stubbles in August/September. Walkers are a problem that has to be suffered. Curiously, the deer probably will not take much notice of them if they stick to known tracks, but with safety in mind you may have to invest in one or two portable high seats. Put them up either where yearlings tend to congregate, or where you know a shootable buck lives. Take the seat away afterwards if there is a risk of vandalism. If you have the chance to volunteer as a beater once or twice next autumn you may get a better idea of the number of deer about and help the keeper too, who may be more flexible about letting you on the ground earlier if he gets more confidence in your dependability.

Reading your debate on whether one ought to leave good bucks until after the rut so that they can pass on their genes, I wonder how important heredity really is in the breeding of fine-antlered bucks. Do they actually pass on their good points, or are other aspects of management more significant?

A man whose knowledge of roe deer was infinitely deeper than mine put it

165

this way: for a buck to grow an exceptional head, he must have been born in a 'vintage year' for kids, have led a comparatively prosperous life and be shot in a 'vintage year' for antler growth. Nothing about who were his parents. My reading of that is that a kid must have a good start in life, reared by a doe in good condition. Through life there must be adequate food and a degree of tranquillity, and that the vintage year for antlers predicates an unusually abundant food supply *through the late-winter growing period.*

The influence of heredity is shown more by the shape of the antlers, rather than their size, so one can see, for example, basic differences between heads from Sussex, Dorset and Scotland. This only shows when you see a collection of heads from one area, rather than individuals.

A buck may have very differently shaped antlers from year to year, and can grow an exceptionally large pair at any age from two to ten years.

A friend locally who does a lot of roe stalking in big forestry plantations tells me that his deer seem to be getting fewer, and what there are have low weights and poor condition. The plantations are getting to the thinning stage and some ride clearance has been done. Can you explain what might be the problem?

One has to do a bit of guesswork, but in your part of the country it's fair to assume that most of the planting was done with sitka spruce, and if thinning is due, that the canopy has closed and there isn't much undergrowth left with the exception of the rides.

For the first fifteen to twenty years after planting, especially on bare heather moorland, an ideal habitat is created with abundant cover and a variety in diet offered by the lush tips of young trees supplemented by all the original herbage. Holding capacity and therefore the roe population is at maximum. Once the ground vegetation is shaded out, the deer have to rely more and more on the lower branches of the growing trees, often marked by a distinct browse line all along the rides. There is still plenty of cover until the pole stage is reached, but little of the varied diet which roe require. Ronnie Rose, that guru of the uplands, once told me that roe deer cannot survive on a diet consisting of more than 75 per cent of sitka needles and I suspect that is at least part of your friend's problem. Another may be that the deer congregate on open patches, left unplanted because they are too boggy, where pond snails and their attendant parasite the liver fluke are likely to infest any roe in the area. Fluke appears to affect young bucks more than does, which can unbalance the sex ratio despite your friend's best efforts.

There seems to be an upsurge in night poaching round here because the price has gone up and I know a number of deer have been taken off my ground in spite of the efforts of local gamekeepers and the police. How can I possibly adjust my cull plans to account for an unknown number that aren't there any more?

Recent research into road accidents involving deer have shown how many are killed annually, often without the owner having any idea of the scale of the problem. Poaching on top of this can make theoretical cull plans meaningless. With road accidents at least many more males than females will be killed, further skewing the figures.

In districts prone to either problem, or both, one has to go back to field counting before each open season in an attempt to discover what is left for the owner or stalker to manage. It is time consuming and with the regrettable extension of the roe doe season, there is no interval in March when this work used to be done as a matter of routine *unless the old close date of the end of February is still observed.*

In the spring the deer tend to be out in the fields and one can not only count their numbers, but note how many does are followed by fawns or, in the case of roe, how many have twins. Maybe there will also be orphans. One can also get an idea of the sex ratio although fallow males tend to separate from the rest at this time of year. Comparing this with an autumn count, an estimate of losses from a variety of causes can be made.

I am trying hard to improve the stock of grouse on my moor, but there a number of roe deer about and they all carry large numbers of ticks. I am afraid they contribute to spreading louping ill which has devastated the grouse. We already put sheep out and dose them regularly with acaricide to act as tick sponges, so would it be a good idea to eliminate the roe?

Ticks, which may carry the viral disease louping ill, can be spread by any of the animals which pick them up: small mammals, mountain hares, sheep and deer. The more movement the greater the risk of spread. However, according to the Game & Wildlife Conservation Trust, roe deer, unlike red deer, cannot act as a reservoir of the disease so your resident roe are not themselves infecting any ticks which bite them. Attempts to eliminate the local stock of deer would be likely to result in a void which would be quickly filled in from outside, thus bringing in more ticks with them. The extra time and trouble involved above what you are already doing by dosing the sheep would be better spent in improving any other factors which may be contributing to holding the grouse population down after one of their periodic crashes – fox and crow control and habitat management in particular. If there are mountain hares on your moor, it might be prudent to take advice on whether they are a significant element in spreading the disease, and whether a reduction in their numbers would be helpful.

Is it possible for one to have an impact on fishtail heads in a wild fallow herd when one only has a portion of their territory. If so, how?

In a park situation it is possible by selective culling more or less to eliminate a tendency in the bucks to grow antlers with divided palms, the so-called 'fishtail' heads, as it does seem to have a genetic origin.

Sadly we continue to mismanage our wild fallow, each landowner or his stalker doing as he pleases, from only shooting the better bucks, or any buck, to indiscriminate killing. Fallow range widely, and may wander over perhaps a seven-mile radius or more in the year.

The only way forward is by collaboration between the many landowners involved and if there is one animal more difficult to manage than the fallow it is we humans. The Deer Initiative (www.thedeerinitiative.co.uk) has been campaigning to promote Local Deer Management Groups. They also offer a FREE Advice Note on Deer Management Groups which is available on their 'downloads' page.

My own experience with such groups suggests that it must consist of the landowners of the area involved or their land agents, not of stalkers, even though they are the ones to do the work. Otherwise there is a risk of it becoming just a stalkers' club without the clout to push through an overall policy which may conflict with their individual interests and is sure to be unpopular with somebody. Because any general interest in fallow is lacking, apart from their status as an agricultural pest, such schemes have some chance of success. In districts where roe predominate, the value of stalking will usually override other considerations and each owner will go his own way regardless.

There is a fallow doe on my farm which is very lame indeed. I think she must have a dislocated hind leg. Would it be kindest to shoot her, and if I do, would it be legal?

You do not say if the doe has a fawn. If she has, there is an additional problem, or even if there is that possibility. I have known deer with crippling injuries which nonetheless managed to mate and rear young.

The Deer Act does allow you to shoot a deer out of season if it is injured or diseased to avoid further suffering, so that much is clear. The ethics are more difficult. If she is obviously dying or in extreme pain, then you have no option, but when fawns are still dependent you should try to find and account for the fawn too. Sadly, the most effective way is to go back to where the doe was shot the following morning when the fawn should be hanging about. This also allows you to ensure that it is not the offspring of a completely different mother. In the event that the injury appears to be not life-threatening and there is a fawn involved, culling might be delayed until the fawn is self-sufficient.

Can one age roe by their teeth?

Once upon a time I thought ageing bucks from their tooth wear was simple. Extract the jawbone, compare the teeth with the excellent illustrations in various current textbooks – and there you were. Unfortunately *'It ain't necessarily so!'* Telling the age of a dead roe is not as difficult as doing the same when it is alive – but nearly.

If a roe still has a three-crowned premolar, it is likely to be less than two years old. This tooth is usually shed in May or thereabouts, at the start of the buck's second year, its two-crowned replacement pushing up from below. Similarly, the third, rearmost, molar only erupts at about that age and is pale and clearly newly emerged for some months afterwards. Anomalies do crop up, but it is a reasonable guide. The teeth of a young deer are high and sharp; through middle age the teeth are ground down by the action of browsing and chewing the cud, wearing the points away and showing larger areas of dark brown dentine. In old age the molars can be worn down so much that they split between the roots, letting them fall out. Once this happens, cudding is incomplete leading to loss of condition. Deer on sandy soils grind their teeth away much quicker than the roe round my home, which is on chalk. Roe spending their lives in the heather, as many do, have to nibble for the forage and a five-year buck may have worn his incisors down to the gums while a chalk-country buck is likely to have his almost unworn at the same age or more.

So, apart from knowing that a roe with milk teeth is a juvenile, how can one get more reliable information from the teeth? One method is to extract the first true molar from a jawbone, saw it down between the roots at right angles to the line of the jaw with a fine hacksaw and polish the surface thus exposed by rubbing it on fine emery. Material is laid down at this point, compensating for wear and raising the tooth in the jaw. Under low magnification and good illumination, lighter and darker bands can be made out in a full-aged beast. Similar to the growth rings in a tree, these do correspond roughly to succeeding seasons, winter bands being darker. In areas where the winters are severe the distinction is more marked. A sharper line may denote a period of scarcity or poor health, or even a specially busy rut!

Deer often come out on the fields round our farmhouse and we like to see them. They are quite big, so I think they must be fallow. Do they get hungry in the winter? Especially round Christmas we do ourselves rather too well and I wonder if we could offer a bit of Christmas cheer to them too? We have plenty of hay.

If the winter is long and severe, deer can have a thin time and may because of this invade gardens and other places where they may not be as welcome as on your farm. It's a pleasant idea to give them the equivalent of a Christmas soup kitchen, but it has to be planned to fit in with their life style and digestion.

If you do decide to go ahead and really try to benefit the deer, it has to be a sustained effort, not just a bale of hay spread out for them on Christmas Eve. Unless they have been picking at hay somewhere, all they will do is lie on it! You can make a small stack in the autumn in a place where they can get to it and roof the stack so that it doesn't spoil. Then they can become used to hay and benefit from it. Don't use bales which have been wrapped in netting – they will get their antlers entangled in it. Also remove baler twine as it gets loosened.

Abroad they make 'leaf hay', which is brushwood such as hazel, cut in the summer in full leaf, allowed to dry naturally and then stacked.

These ideas could make a happier Christmas for your deer in the future. I have to say that it might be all too successful – and you get more visitors than you bargain for!

A correspondent rang me the other day wanting advice. Did I remember that plantation of Corsican pine with a high seat at each corner? Getting grown-in and difficult. His unusually long-sighted Forester has given him permission to drive a clearing straight through it in the name of deer control; how is he to make such a major concession as effective as possible?

In this example there is every reason for not letting the clearing extend out to the surrounding rides: in these days of public access the casual walker is less willing to penetrate a good tangle of conifer and bramble. You are not making a picnic place! Also the whole thing is warmer and more secret without the winds of heaven sweeping from one end to the other. So make sure that clearance ends ten yards short of any ride **and be there when they do the work to ensure that such a strange notion is actually carried out!** Access for a tractor can be via an unobtrusive wandering diagonal track between the trees otherwise the picnic party is likely to be held in the seat, or some Anti who cares more about animals than people may find it and sabotage the ladder rungs!

Ideally a clearing should be pear-shaped about 100 yards long by maximum 30 wide, the narrow part overlooked by a high seat. Planting game-attractive crops is practised widely on the Continent, but it is inevitably a costly performance needing renewing every year. Under the conditions in southern England at least, it is infinitely cheaper, and probably as effective, to provide low-growing coppice growth for the deer. If almost any broadleaved species (except birch) has to be cut down to make the clearing, the regrowth makes extremely attractive browse. All that needs then to be done is to organise an annual cut by swipe or flail mower of *half the area*. If one side is done one year and the opposite side the next, there will always be about knee-high scrub consisting mostly of deer-attractive plants. Shooting will still be possible from the high seats. In the absence of good browse, or to enhance it, the easiest browse to plant in most situations is willow. One species or another will grow in most situations and almost all of them are beloved by deer, not only as browse, but for fraying too. If at any stage they get in the way of forest operations, then they can be cut off. The regrowth will be even more of an attraction! Knowing the way deer seek out anything unusual, try to choose one that is not universal in the wood: if goat willow is abundant, go for an osier. In hill districts where grey or oval-eared willow occur, try to get some goat willow plants. All of them are easy to propagate: take finger-thickness green sticks in March about twelve inches long, push them into the soil until only four inches show, and let them root. Covering the new plant with some brush stops the deer eating the shoots before the tree has had a chance to become established.

My ground is poor and sandy, planted with sitka spruce, and the deer don't hang about on the forestry rides. Can one improve the vegetation somehow to tempt them out?

If the rides locally are naturally grass covered, which often means poor soil, a bucket of fertiliser spread by hand a couple of times a year makes the resulting vegetation more toothsome. In really poor upland areas dominated by molinia, a really hard low cut by swipe late in the summer promotes late growth which will bring the deer out on that bit of ride.

10 Trophies and trophy preparation

Deer antlers have a deep fascination for many of us. We even decorate our homes with skulls which, unless periodically dusted, become the abode of spiders, a source of domestic disharmony. What is it about them? An unassuming roe head can hardly be thought of as a status symbol like a valuable picture or a BMW in the front drive, but it's a matter of pride to the chap who shot it, and even sometimes to others.

A trophy is something intensely personal, whether it is a tiny pin feather from a woodcock proudly pushed into your hatband or a mounted moose head looming over your dining table. Either conjures up some moment of intense emotion and is as thrilling to the owner in retrospect as it is desperately boring to anybody else.

Deer antlers have a unique interest because of their infinite variety – every one is different. Just a glance at a roe head I shot more than fifty years ago gives an instant mental picture of the place, the difficulties of the stalk and the shot, even the weather at the time. No diary or fading photograph in a long-neglected album could do that.

In addition, because they are grown quickly, antlers reflect the well-being of the animal and so a series from one place can be a good indicator of how well the herd has been managed over years.

Your souvenir must be properly presented and tended – the skull white, antlers clean and never allowed to get dusty or cobwebbed. Not everyone likes their heads mounted on shields, but if they are, no ugly screw-heads must show from the front.

When they have shot a nice head, most stalkers want to know whether it is 'good', but this is where the problems arise because what is fantastic in one area may be run-of-the-mill elsewhere. However, some objective standards can be applied as a guide, and this is where the CIC trophy measuring service comes in. An accredited trophy judge will apply a given set of criteria (the formula) to arrive at a score of so many points. The purpose is not to let you say 'My head is better than yours', but to see how it is placed against an international standard. The result of measuring a large number of heads annually has also shown, for example, that letting the stalking of trophy bucks has not generally affected the quality of our roe.

No one who was in the BDS tent at the CLA Game Fair at Broadlands in 2006 could mistake the enormous interest in the two notable roe heads which were brought in for measurement. Likewise, by the crowds clustering round the CIC trophy judges at work at the four Game Fairs, one can have no doubt how important it is to many stalkers to find out how their heads compare to an international standard. An onlooker might take this interest as some kind of competition, but in fact that is not true. If a trophy reaches a pre-set number of points, it is judged to be of gold, silver or bronze standard. Quite apart from the interest to the stalker concerned, encouraging stalkers to come forward with their heads has a variety of very valuable functions. First, as antler growth is an indicator of the well-being of a deer species, a long-term decline among the heads measured would signal some deterioration in management. Fortunately the reverse is true in the case of both roe and muntjac – quite apart from those two 'record' heads, the number of first-class heads recorded annually has been increasing steadily. Without the trophy-measuring service, the old argument that pay-stalking was creaming off all the best roebucks with disastrous results could not be proved untrue. In contrast, our mismanaged wild fallow deer are seldom allowed to achieve antlers which compare with those from other countries.

Eager gatherings at Game Fairs are also a fine opportunity for the exchange of ideas between stalkers who would lack the chance in the normal course of a lonely occupation. In a less spectacular way, the flow of house visits to the seven trophy judges through the year has a similar value and also brings in information which otherwise might be lost. Yes – we delight in our trophies as souvenirs of exciting stalks and wonderful country enjoyed at its best at dusk and dawn, but each head is so individual in looks and associations that one can never claim 'Mine is better than yours!' In true sports, as contrasted with games, there should be no competition. So decorate yours with tinsel at Christmas, or hang a gold CIC medal round it as respect for a fallen opponent. And share the delight of a fellow stalker with his own trophies without a trace of envy – if you can!

The questions that follow show how deep is the interest in trophies among stalkers.

Trophy preparation

This year I am intending to prepare my own trophy buck heads, but am unsure how to do this.

The main thing is to cut the buck's head off quickly and put it in a bucket of cold water. It will be fine overnight; if longer – change the water. Try not to put it in the freezer – they take ages to defrost.

As soon as you can, slit the skin from under the throat to the nose and then peel it upwards, being careful not to score the bone. Free round the pedicles and cut the skin away. At this stage decide how you want to show your trophy – either with the whole skull, less lower jaw, with the palate cut away below the eye sockets ('long nose cut') or from the articulation with the top vertebra through the centre of the eye sockets ('standard cut'). If you want to cut the skull, now is the time. It is easier to clean if you make a straight cut from the articulation of the top vertebra out to the nose with a woodsaw, then you can scrape out the brain before boiling. When you get it measured eventually, you lose a few points by doing that, rather than cleaning the whole skull, but if it is your first attempt, I'd suggest you do.

Hinge the lower jaw downwards and it will disconnect. Lay the skull on its side, preferably with a block under the nose, and cut with a woodsaw half-way through. Then look to see if you are going straight. If not, don't try to change direction of the cut, but start again from the other side, making a botch in the middle where it won't be seen.

Put the skull in a saucepan and fill with water up to the base of the coronets – not higher. If your pan is not aluminium, put in a tablespoonful of washing soda to help things on. Boil carefully until the flesh starts to peel away from the bone, older bucks take longer. Then you either start scraping away with a not-too-sharp stalking knife or if you have access to a pressure washer, one of those will take most of the flesh off and clean out the brain cavity, but it's a messy business and you need full protective clothing!

One way or the other, when you have removed all the flesh and soft tissue, cover the bone (but not the antlers) with cotton wool or tissues and soak it in domestic hydrogen peroxide. Use rubber gloves. Leave overnight and your trophy should emerge nicely white and when dry will not smell.

If you need more detail, you will find it in my book *Roe Deer – Management and Stalking*, (Swan Hill Press – www.countrybooksdirect.com), page 129 onwards.

With the trophy question in mind, I wonder if you would mind giving me your thoughts on this query please. I have a very fine roe trophy I culled on 7 June which I hope to get measured after the obligatory three-month drying period, but during boiling out the cradle holding the skull slipped and the some of the pedicles have been bleached (mostly on the rear). Will this bleaching null and void the score or will it just be a loss to the overall total?

It is a very fine set, very symmetrical with six fine points and nice pearling. If this does score enough to be a medal it will be a first from 'my patch'.

Alas, I know too well what happened while you were boiling out your trophy! You got a white patch and a high-tide mark of scum. The best device for avoiding this problem I have found is a multi-jointed clamp which attaches to the antler at one end and the rim of the saucepan at the other. You can get one from Bushwear (www.bushwear.co.uk).

Even now you have that discolouration all is not lost *provided you don't attempt to do anything about it until it has been judged.* You just lose a point or two for colour, whereas if there is any artificial colouring, you lose all four. Some people like to smarten up their heads in a variety of ways – emery cloth on the points or teak oil on the beams. It's entirely up to the stalker – the buck won't care, being dead. Various dyes have been used, such as permanganate of potash or boot polish, besides artists' colours. I notice that the Bushwear catalogue lists some special antler dye as well as other useful trophy preparation products from Germany among other specialised kit for stalkers. They also sell a variety of wooden shields which can sometimes be difficult to run to earth. Ring 0845 226 0469 for a catalogue.

My personal preference is to leave them in their natural state. It's just important to restrain oneself until after the judgement has been made.

To avoid boiling water bleaching the antlers, a handy clamp holds the skull in the right position.

175

I have shot a fine wild goat and want to mount it on a shield, but the tips of the horns touch the wall behind. How do I get over this, and is there a formula for measuring them, like there is for deer? How do I get it measured?

When you have cut the skull in any way you like to see it, offer it up to the wall and block out the back of the skull until the points are clear. Then cut a wedge to that thickness to go between the skull and the shield. This should do the trick.

There is a measuring formula, involving taking the width, and the circumference progressively up each horn. Medals are awarded as they are for deer. Medal levels have recently been updated, and these are now: Bronze 250–299.9; Silver 300–349.9 and Gold 350 upwards. A good head should be in the region of 70 cm (27 inches) long.

CIC trophy judges attend four Game Fairs annually, or they can be contacted through their website www.cictrophy.com

There are some old red deer heads on the gable end of this house and some roe on a shed. I would like to bring some inside for ornament, but they are rather bleached and the bone is covered with lichen. Is there any way of reviving them?

If the heads are really old and weathered, you have quite a job to make those heads look presentable at short range. If they haven't been there that long, there is quite a bit you can do.

If the antlers are just bleached (and it's surprising how quickly this happens, even while still attached to the original owner) then the colour can be restored by careful application of teak oil followed by a careful brushing with dark brown boot polish. Red deer antlers usually look better with the tips of the tines left white and repolished by rubbing with very fine steel wool, grading it off into the coloured part. If it is very well pearled, any colouring can be gently removed from the tops of the pearls, as it would be in life. After several years nature leaches away the wax from the antlers leaving them porous and you may need to replace this in addition to colouring and polishing. I have used warm boot wax for the purpose, but this is getting into artistry rather than restoration.

The skull part with the pedicles will also need attention. Often it has become brittle and porous. Scrubbing with warm water and detergent will make a start, using a wire brush to get lichen and bird droppings off. Bleach is unlikely to do much good at this stage, the stains have gone too deep. The most practical solution is likely to be a thin coat of off-white matt emulsion paint.

If the heads are mounted on shields, these can be stripped, stained and finished in the normal way if the wood is still sound.

Looking at a friend's collection of deer heads, I noticed that some roe and one fallow had a very rough surface to the bone of the forehead. One of the roe had a malformed set of antlers. Is this just age, or is it caused by some disease?

This roughening of the bone is caused by damage to the periosteum, the membrane between skin and bone which carries blood vessels and nerves for the nutrition and development of the bones. When it is irritated an increased deposit of bone takes place beneath it, and this is what you have seen.

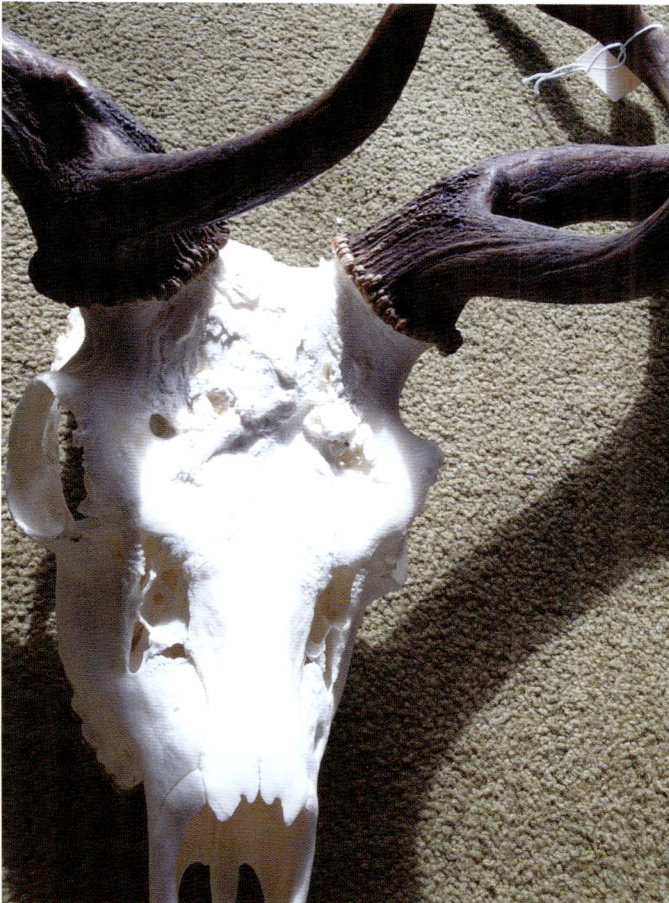

Roughening of the forehead bone follows injury caused by fighting or infestation by greenbottle larvae.

Male deer are inevitably the worst sufferers. Probably the damage starts when the animals fight, the forehead and top of the skull taking most of the impact. The impact alone may be enough to give rise to inflammation of the periosteum. If the skin is ruptured greenbottle flies *Lucilia caesar* are attracted which lay their eggs in the wound. This is the same insect, similar to a bluebottle but metallic green, which causes 'fly-strike' in sheep. Larvae hatch and begin burrowing into the surrounding tissues, mainly round the coronets where the unfortunate beast is unable to get at them. They may even eat away the skull to expose the brain. It is a disgusting sight to encounter a badly affected buck, which will be in obvious distress, shaking its head and wandering aimlessly about. In roe there seems to be a connection between this and the later development of a malformed head, although the fly-strike will have occurred in summer, six months before the new set of antlers is grown. Even if the beast survives, the extra bone laid down persists and shows up when the skull is boiled out.

My son has shot a decent stag, which has been prepared as a bare skull. How do I do about getting it mounted on a shield for him?

There are three approaches to this problem depending on your budget and your own handicraft abilities. There are now plenty of working taxidermists who would do the job, maybe with a bit of delay because on the whole they are busy people these days. Contact the Taxidermists' Guild (www.taxidermy.org.uk) or www.touchlocal.com/business/search/typeId/1949/type/Taxidermists for a list of addresses.

Alternatively, given basic skills with a screwdriver, get hold of Bushwear's catalogue (www.bushwear.co.uk)or phone them on 0845 226 0469 to discover the selection of shields they have on offer.

With reasonable DIY facilities it is pretty straightforward to make a simple shield out of seasoned wood about two centimetres thick and slightly longer than the skull, using a jigsaw to cut the curves to any shape which pleases the eye, bevelling the edges and sanding the surface. Hardwoods look good just polished, softwood probably needs a coat or two of clear varnish. To hang it, triangular brass 'glass plates' with a keyhole at the top can be bought at any hardware shop, then drill one screw-hole in the shield, countersunk at the back. This needs to be placed so that a woodscrew can reach and secure to the bridge of bone between the eye sockets. Bore a small hole in this to give the screw a lead. For a red deer you will need something like a no.14 woodscrew. Doing it this way there are no unsightly screw heads on the frontal bone. If this is too much of a challenge, a local joiner will probably have the materials and equipment to produce a blank for you to finish if you give him a paper pattern of the size and shape you have in mind.

Trophy measurement

A chum of mine shot what he thinks is a big roebuck in the rut in early August. Can you tell me what to look for to make a 'trophy' buck, and where he should apply to get a definite answer?

Beauty is in the eye of the beholder. The main thing about a memorable trophy is that the stalk should have been exciting. Some of the bucks I remember best had nothing much in the way of big antlers, but something about getting each one stays with one for ever. That's a real trophy! However, it is interesting to know how a buck measures up against international standards and the days of having to exhibit one's precious head at a distant foreign exhibition are long gone.

There are one or two starting points for knowing whether a head is likely to make the charts: first, the skull must be properly boiled out and dry. A skull loses about 10 per cent of its weight in the first few weeks after boiling out. Don't glue it to the shield or fill the skull cavity with anything, as the nett weight is critical.

For a long time now, deer heads have been judged using formulae developed by the CIC (The International Council for Game and Wildlife Conservation), originally for large-scale exhibitions which were organised every ten years. It's not a competition, so the award of a medal depends on the points scored, not whether it is the best out of a number of others. The likely sizes of a trophy of the various game species found in the U K are set out on the following page.

Besides the normal system of phone appointments for measuring, CIC trophy judges normally attend the CIC and Midland Game Fairs, and for Scotland at Scone and Moy either in the British Deer Society or Forestry Commission stands. To get more information log on to the CIC United Kingdom Permanent Trophy Commission website (www.cictrophy.com).

I am thinking of bringing some of my trophies to one of the Game Fairs this summer to get them measured. Can you give me some idea of how to choose the ones which are likely to be in the medal class?

One can only give general guidance, as obviously much depends on the appearance of an individual trophy. However, for the various UK species, these minimum figures should give some sort of guide:

Red stag: Ten points or more, with long brow and trey points and long crown points or shorter if numbering more than eight. Length 90 cm; with heavy beams; weight of skull 5 kg. Lower medal levels are quoted for wild Scottish stags.

Fallow buck: The formula for this species is complex, relying on wide, unsplit palmation and good spellers. Length (to top of palm) 60 cm; width of palm 15 cm; palm length 35 cm.

Roe buck: Weight: depends on how the skull has been cut: if cut through the eye sockets (short nose) a head with normal tines weighing 360+ grams (12 ounces) is likely to come into the bronze category. Silver needs about 420 and gold 470 grams. For long-nose cuts add 60 grams and for a full skull add 90 grams. These are very approximate, and only give a general guide as there are beauty points and other variations that affect the final score to a greater extent than with other species.

Muntjac buck: symmetry and strength of the beams and the presence of two brows are important points. Length needs to be around 10 cm (4 inches) or more.

Japanese sika stag: Again, symmetry is very important. A even eight- or ten-pointer is desirable. Length 50 cm; span 40 cm; brows and treys 14 cm; upper point 7 cm.

Chinese water deer buck: The tusks must be detached from the skull. Length 75 mm total length round the curve; 28 mm circumference at point of eruption from the gum.

Wild boar: Length of lower tusks 20cm. These and the 'grinders' (upper tusks) need to be strong and worn so that the brown dentine shows a good length.

Feral goat: Length 65 cm. The type with wide-spreading horns has an advantage over those with narrow span.

Muntjac and sika heads can be measured even if they have been fully mounted, but roe, red and fallow need to be bare skull without any additions such as a block in the skull or dye on the antlers. Skulls need to be fully dried.

How long does a roe trophy need to dry out before it can be measured? Most of my stalking clients want to take their heads back with them, but they still want medals if their trophies qualify. Does a skull lose much weight after it is boiled out and reasonably dry?

To answer your last question first, a roe head loses about 10 per cent of its weight between 24 hours after boiling out and three months, although most of this is lost in the first week. For this reason, to qualify for an official score and the prestigious CIC medal that can go with it, a three-month interval after boiling is imposed to make sure it is completely dry. For muntjac, sika and Chinese water deer trophies, where weight is not an element, the three-month delay may now be waived.

To cope with the difficulty where visiting stalkers need to take their heads home after a stalking holiday, CIC UK Trophy Commission trophy judges can issue a provisional score for recently shot heads which are properly boiled out and reasonably dry. For qualifying heads UK Trophy Commission medals of bronze, silver and gold are available against this provisional score.

My best roe trophy has just been measured and turns out to be a Gold Medal. I'm a bit sore because if I had known, I would have had it mounted head and shoulders but of course I threw away the skin and cut the skull.

Is there anything I can do now?

I sympathise, but the situation is not lost. Most taxidermists don't use all the skull anyway, and it should be possible to get another skin. Make contact with a taxidermist, and look at some of his work to make sure you like the way he mounts roe. Get a quote for the work. Tell him what you have in mind, and he will brief you about how to skin and preserve the new cape. Whatever you do, don't cut up the underside of the neck as you would normally – that's the bit everyone looks at when it is on the wall. The taxidermist will probably ask you to cut round well behind the shoulders and peel the front half of the skin towards and up the neck like a sock, cutting off the head still with the skin attached, and putting the whole thing as quickly as possible into the freezer. Wait until the bucks are in good summer coat next season, and try to find a cull buck of roughly the same age for your substitute. The final result will look super!

In this year's English review I note that two heads beat the long-standing record. It also states that MP White's roe head is also the UK record for length at an average of 31.9 cm. I have in front of me a copy of Richard Prior's Modern Roe Stalking *in which it states that the longest recorded British roebuck measured 34 cm. It was shot by B de Buday-Goldberger in Sussex in 1968. 'This may also be a world record for length for a European roe.' So who holds the record for antler length?*

The answer to your first question is quite straightforward – Bertie de Buday-Goldberger's roebuck, which I have to say was one of the most beautiful heads

One antler of a Sussex buck shot in 1968 is possibly the longest recorded at 34 cm, but taking the average of both, as is accepted nowadays, at 31.9 cm. Marco Pierre White's Hampshire buck exceeds it.

I have ever seen, quite apart from its unusual length, did measure 34 cm, but this was on one side only. Marco-Pierre White's buck had an *average* length of 31.9 cm and as we take the average these days, it does stand as the record.

As to the European record for length, it is quite possible that a buck with exceptionally long antlers did not match in other ways, and therefore would not have qualified as a gold medal, for which records are kept. On a quick look through the catalogues for the last two big International Trophy Exhibitions, at Budapest in 1971 and Plovdiv in 1981, roe heads averaging over 30 cm are pretty scarce: twelve at Budapest out of some thousands listed, and only three at Plovdiv. The longest of those exhibited was a buck shot in Romania in 1959 which measured 35.0 and 36.2 cm, and this was the only trophy listed which exceeded Marco Pierre White's Hampshire buck.

The International Council for Game and Wildlife Conservation (CIC) preserves records of notable heads of all European species, but these records are kept in a university library. It may be possible to access them through their website: www.cic-wildlife.org

Where does one purchase these thin tape measures that you use to measure heads? I am told they are called diameter tape measures, but the best tool shop locally tell me they have never heard of them.

The CIC rules for trophy measuring specify a flat metal tape, one-quarter inch wide, and indeed we do use engineers' diameter tapes for the purpose, which are very expensive and also difficult to track down, as you have found. They have the advantage that there is a blank length at the end rather than the usual type with a small, rather mobile hook at 0 cm, which is less precise.

However, for amateur use to arrive at an approximation of the CIC score and to see whether a head is likely to make the charts if sent up to a trophy judge, a variety of household tapes can be used. It is best to avoid cloth tapes, however, as they are often found to be very inaccurate and fit into all the corrugations of pearling, which is not allowed. Metal tapes which are concave and semi-rigid are very difficult to use. Rather than this, you can use a length of fairly limp plastic- or paper-coated garden tying wire, marking on it the length as measured and then laying it out against a ruler to establish the length.

If there is any question of measuring the trophies of stalking clients, stalkers who do not live close to a trophy judge and whose clients want to take their heads home with them are very well advised to steer clear of basing their charges on CIC ratings. Visitors are all too likely to get them re-measured when they get home – and woe betide the stalker if the final score happens to be lower!

I have just shot a Chinese water deer buck with nice tusks. I would like to get

them measured, but how do I get them out undamaged? How long do the teeth have to be to get them into a possible medal category?

Chinese water deer tusks are curious in that they grow in a pad of gristle and are slightly movable. This is probably so that they can be used as a weapon, but otherwise hinge back not to get in the way of grazing. They have to be extracted in order to be measured to the CIC formula, and it is easy to damage them. Paul Taylor, the Dorset taxidermist, happened to call in, so I was able to get the best advice. He recommends boiling out the head thoroughly and de-fleshing it, preferably with a pressure hose if you have one, particularly directing the jet round the tusk sockets. Then *while the skull is still wet and warm*, the tusks can be wriggled out.

Provided both tusks are intact and roughly the same length, they need to be about 70 mm in length and around 29 mm circumference at the point of eruption from the gum.

Can you tell me how many medal-class roe trophies are shot in the United Kingdom each year? The total must compare very favourably with many other European countries.

Replying to your query about the number of medal roe shot each year, unfortunately we just don't know. Quite a few get taken abroad by visiting stalkers and we don't see them. Others, of course, just don't get presented for measurement. It's a pity, because the greater the number we see and record each year, the better and more valuable the data base for looking at the effects of current culling on the health and condition of the deer year by year.

Between England and Scotland the details of an average of 137 gold medal heads are given in the *Shooting Times & Country Magazine* 'Roe Review', itself no mean indication that the excellent quality of our roe deer is being maintained. Most stalkers nowadays have a fair idea of the levels required to achieve the various medal categories, and so many good bucks which are less likely to score highly are kept by the owners, but not presented, so one might guess that at least as many silver medal heads are being taken, and a larger number of bronze. Other countries have more rigid rules which enforce the registration of all trophies and so their information is more comprehensive. However, Britain has a premier position in the quality of our roe and I would be the last person to suggest that stricter documentation would be desirable or necessary! Even the published figures demonstrate very clearly country-wide that critics of letting stalking of mature bucks are on very shaky ground. Though cases of local over-shooting have come to light, the speed with which trophy quality and therefore stalking revenue goes down soon points to their basic error.

Is it safe to send my precious roe head by post for you to measure? If so, what advice can you give to make sure it comes back in one piece?

I have plenty of heads sent by post every year and haven't yet had a real disaster, touch wood. Sometimes one has arrived with the points sticking out, but this is because too small a box has been chosen in the first place. Find one with *plenty* of room all round and pack the skull and antlers round with tightly balled newspaper so that the whole box is quite full with no movement possible. A good wrapping of parcel tape makes all shipshape. Enclose details of the head, that is, your name, address and phone number – this is so that I can let you know the good news – also the date the buck was shot, and the county. If you are sending it on behalf of a visiting stalker, make it clear who is to be credited.

The parcel should be dispatched by Special Delivery, or at least Signed For. If the first, let me know when to expect it so that someone is here to take delivery.

Footnote
An interesting example of continuing affection for a trophy came to light recently. Mr CP Brown wrote to me enclosing a photograph of some antlers which have been in his family for more than fifty years. They belonged to a buck which was found dead on the north side of Croydon Hill, near Minehead in Somerset in 1953 – a time when roe deer were not known to exist on Exmoor. It was thought that it could have been a victim of the disastrous floods which led to the Lynmouth disaster in 1952. This appears to be a fully mature, six-point buck, probably quite old.

As reported in *Country Life*:

One or two people, when told of this find, were incredulous and the existence of roe within six miles of Minehead was not generally known. I have as yet met no one who knew or suspected that roe had spread into these traditional haunts of red deer, though it would seem almost impossible that roe could live and breed here without hunt servants or gamekeepers becoming aware of their presence.

This was not strictly true, as even then there was a roe head hanging in the bar of the inn at Exford with, I seem to remember, an inscription saying that it had been hunted and taken in 1937. Maybe some reader will correct the details. So even then occasional roe were travelling away from their

A picture of the 'Lynmouth Disaster' buck, with the grouse and blackgame which still existed on Exmoor in those days. The family decorates the antlers with tinsel every Christmas.

known haunts on the Devon/Dorset border. My own first buck was taken in 1953 near Honiton, thirty miles off as the crow flies, and they were pretty scarce even there. My correspondent's parents, who found the buck, recalled being alarmed at night hearing a roe barking near their home at Rodhuish. This was years before the area was fully colonised.

They salvaged the antlers, had them mounted on a plaque and a local artist, sadly anonymous, not only painted the head, but embellished the sketch with a roebuck, a pair of black game and a red grouse. Both these game birds existed in the area at that time. It was titled *Antlers of Roe Deer from dead buck found at the foot of Black Hill, Nov. 1952.*

The trophy has become a prized possession of the family. Mr Brown tells me that it has always been decorated with tinsel as part of the Christmas celebrations.

11 The various column

In any game book the various column sometimes records the most interesting or unusual events in a day's shooting on the lines of '189 pheasants & a large rat' or my grandfather's laconic note in his field diary for 1877: 'Went perch fishing and shot a tabby cat.' Always something to quote at a sleepy Women's Institute talk to make them sit up! While a deer stalker's diary is unlikely to show much variation in the actual bag, though much of interest otherwise, odd events do crop up which might qualify under the 'various' heading. My old friend Kenneth Macarthur was phoned early one morning by an agitated housewife in Dumfries who said that a large striped animal was eating her chickens. Ken, somewhat dubious, turned out to see what was the trouble – and indeed encountered a large raccoon in the act of polishing off another hen. Definitely various. There was also the celebrated report of 'super-squirrels' damaging trees in South Devon. They turned out to be porcupines!

My own mixed bag of Sporting Answers in the *Shooting Times & Country Magazine* is more modest, but always interesting.

Wild boar

Wild boar seem to be spreading in several counties and look like a very attractive new quarry species for stalkers, besides the need to control them. Is a normal stalking rifle, such as a .243 or .270 powerful enough? Do I have to have it mentioned on my FAC, or are they covered by the term 'vermin'?

The last is an interesting query, and rather a grey area as we haven't had wild boar in this country since the Middle Ages. The official view is that they are not vermin and so my advice is to play safe and get a variation on your certificate.

A full-grown boar is a formidable beast with heavy bone, especially in the skull, and very thick solid skin on its neck. They are tenacious of life, even with a mortal wound. Although they are normally shy animals, a wounded boar is a very serious adversary, likely to attack using its tusks and great strength. One needs to use 'enough gun' as the old-time big-game hunters said. Of course boar can be killed by stalking rifles, but a heavily

Numbers of wild boar now exist in several parts of England. They are likely to be a future pest but need care if stalkers are not to be injured by them. PHOTO: B PHIPPS

built, slow-expanding bullet is needed for penetration. Opinion among Continental stalkers favours not less than 7 x 64 (.270) and for driven situations where the risk of a misplaced shot is higher, 8 mm or much larger calibres are often used. In our terms, either the .308 or 30-06 with one of the heavier bullets available would be a good choice, without the need for buying a special weapon for what must still be a very occasional chance.

I hear that there are a number of wild boar breeding in the wild these days. Are they likely to find and eat roe and muntjac fawns?

In spite of a bland assurance on a BBC programme that wild boar are vegetarians, they are omnivorous and would have no hesitation in eating a ground-nesting bird and its eggs or young or any small or juvenile mammals up to hedgehog size which they come across and which are not quick enough to escape. Anyone who has found himself trying to shoot driven birds in a piggery knows that you have to be smart retrieving the fallen before they are polished off by the sows! In Continental Europe where deer and boar co-exist, nobody I have spoken to seemed too worried about fawn losses from boar acting as predators, although they would undoubtedly act as scavengers, eating any carcasses and probably killing any wounded, ill or moribund deer they find. They are known to catch and eat roe kids in the first few weeks of life. We have relatively high populations of roe and muntjac in this country. Boar have good noses, and as they become more numerous here may well develop a strategy of searching out young deer which are not old enough to escape.

I have been told that there are wild boar in the woods locally where local people, including myself, like to walk and exercise our dogs. Are they very dangerous, either to walkers or dogs? Are they likely to do damage if they get into the gardens?

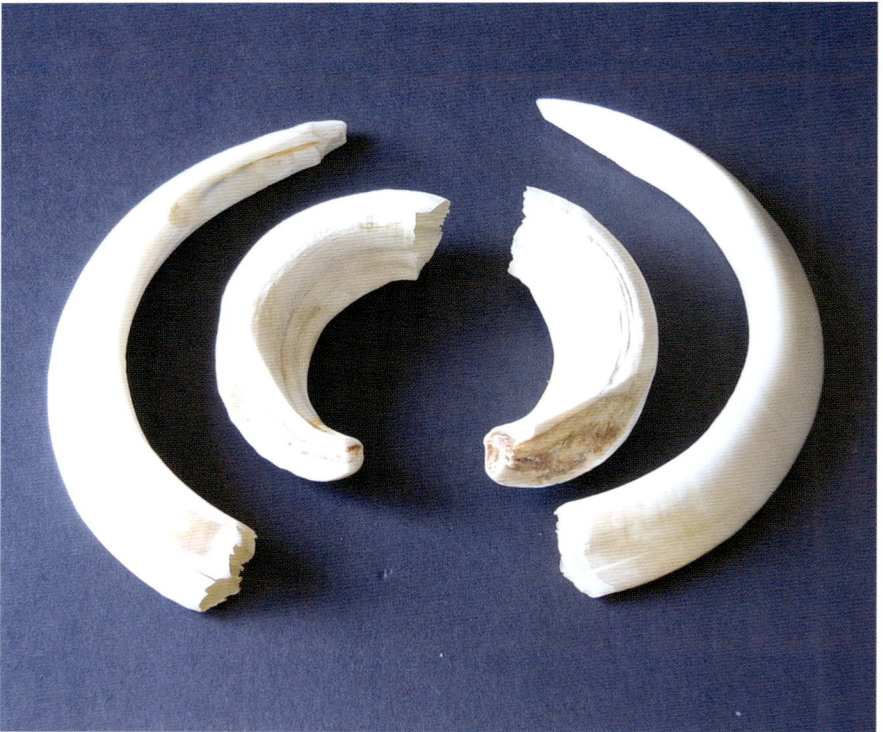

A mature boar has formidable tusks and is quick to use them if annoyed.

Wild boar are spreading at quite a rate from various places in this country. They have escaped from farms where they are kept for meat. Mature males can weigh as much as 150 kg (330 pounds) and are formidably armed with tusks. If frightened or wounded they can be dangerous. One slash, often taken high on the leg, can result from a boar's panic flight or indeed a deliberate charge. However, under normal conditions they are very shy beasts, adept at keeping out of sight. The usual evidence of their arrival is the way they dig with their snouts, producing runs of disturbed turf similar to but much deeper than those produced by badgers, which is annoying to the farmer and much worse for the owner of a golf course – or a garden.

Boar are predominately nocturnal. On average the sows produce one litter of four to six piglets a year, mostly in the spring, sometimes a second in autumn when food is plentiful, and these are the times when a casual walker or especially a loose dog may stumble across a breeding sow who will defend herself and her piglets. Her bite would be unpleasant for a human, and possibly fatal to a dog.

So to answer your question, walkers are very unlikely to come to close quarters with a wild boar, or suffer more than surprise and possibly pleasure at an unusual sight, however, where they are present, keep your dogs on the lead and don't let your children rampage off recognised footpaths, which the boar in general will avoid.

Dogs

A well-trained dog is, no doubt of it, the deer stalker's ultimate insurance policy. If a beast goes off after the shot and can't immediately be found, then one has the need and the moral obligation to make use of a dog's nose, speed and experience to make sure that deer is found and if necessarily, humanely dispatched. At that moment there is enormous relief and also satisfaction, especially if you trained the dog yourself.

There are other advantages too: companionship for only one. Stalking in company with one of the pointing breeds is an education as all the scents come to his nose from upwind, to be conveyed by subtle flicks of the ears, stiffening of the whole body and so on. My own Labrador would sit endlessly while I finished a tricky stalk, or crawl with me, belly to ground. There was a silly scene in front of a film crew where I was supposed to make a cautious stalk, sit the dog with a single hand movement, peer through some bushes and appear to take a shot. All went well up to the point where the dog was supposed to be gestured to sit – at which there was laughter from the back because seeing me commence a stalk, she had sat down by the camera.

Despite all this, I have some unwilling thoughts about having a dog with you because all of your attention ought to be concentrated on the stalk while inevitably a slice of that has to be sacrificed towards attending to the dog, what it is thinking and doing. Real still hunting in the full meaning of the phrase means an almost trance-like state of utter awareness of the wood and what stirs in it. I do not think one can achieve that state with any companion, human or canine. But come to the end – you can't leave poor Bonzo in the car, nor can you do without him when that fatal moment arrives when you really need him. As I used to tell mine when all had gone banana-shaped 'Go on! Find it! That's what I pay you for.'

As a keen stalker I can see the need for a trained dog to find shot deer. I have always loved beagles and have a promising puppy I intend to train. Are there any points you can suggest?

The natural habit of beagles, like any hound, is to nose out and chase their quarry, so trying to train your beagle as a stalking companion is likely to be

Stalking with a well-trained German short-haired pointer.

Every stalker should own a trained deer dog, or have a contact with someone who does in the event of a deer being lost.

a frustrating job. I have seen beagles used in this country and in Sweden to move roe, but even for this which is natural to them, they are extremely difficult to control. You may start out looking for deer, but after that it's more likely you will be looking for beagles for the rest of the day!

In Continental Europe there is a very keen following of those who interest themselves in deer dogs, holding training sessions and eventually field trials for this special purpose. There are primarily two distinct disciplines in which deer dogs are trained: either you have a dog with you while stalking to point deer by scent and then to find dead or wounded deer soon after the shot, or if a deer has been known to be wounded or lost, breeds with very keen noses are employed after hours or even days to track and find them.

For the first category the HPR (hunt–point–retrieve) breeds are favoured, especially the German short-haired and wire-haired pointers, the Weimaraner and the Hungarian Vizsla. Although these are multi-purpose breeds, deer work is an integral part of their formal training. For long-term tracking and finding dead game, the Hanovarian and Bavarian bloodhounds are outstanding. Slightly separate from this are the Scandinavian elkhounds, which are used to locate elk (moose) and bring them to bay to be approached and shot by the hunter, or afterwards located if the shot was not immediately fatal.

Teckels, working dachshunds, are very useful in tracking wounded game, generally being used on a long leash. Being small, they can be carried up into a high seat, but they rely on hunting ability rather than speed to account for anything which is still mobile that a longer-legged breed might run down.

Most of these breeds are already well established in this country, but many stalkers in Britain use our own gundog breeds, of which the Labrador is the most common because they are so biddable. However, their body language is not so easy to 'read' as, for example, that of a German short-haired pointer, whose every quiver sends messages to its handler.

I have known some English springers and border terriers which were good at the job, which speaks volumes for their handlers! There was even a miniature long-haired dachs called Chloe who lived in the fur muff affected by some lady shooters on winter boar drives abroad. In fact Chloe was no lapdog, as I found when I saw her released from the muff, take up the trail of a wounded boar and joyfully join in the scrimmage when it was finally located.

All regular stalkers should own a dog trained to deer. If the choice falls on one of the HPR breeds or a Labrador, deer work does not prevent your dog being a steady and valuable small-game finder and retriever as well.

I am trying to train my Labrador to find shot deer. He has a good nose and if he sees the animal fall, is on it very quickly. If it has disappeared without him seeing it, he just runs in circles and could be rabbiting. If he does finally find it, I don't know where he is, and he just comes back with some blood on his nose, looking pleased. Is the answer to have him on a long string, or what?

Your Lab is hunting on the breast-high scent, which blows off the deer and may lie yards downwind from the actual line the deer took. To train a dog to put its nose down and spell out the real line, you need to train it on a scent trail laid *downwind* so that the air scent has blown off. My experience of following a blood trail with my dog on a long line ended in a cat's cradle, with me on one end, the dog on the other, and a tangle of bushes in between. I expect the line is still there! After that, I used a small bell (a three-inch tourist cowbell from Interlaken) on a collar which only went on when there was a deer to find. At least one could follow the noise and have some idea where the hunt was going. It's wonderful to train a dog to 'bark dead' and stay with the beast until you get there, but failing that, one has to run to keep the tinkle of the bell in hearing, and hope to catch up before long. It's not a perfect solution, but I am not a very good dog trainer! No doubt you can do better.

I have a Labrador who is quite good at finding deer which have run off after the shot, but if I can't get to him in thick cover, he comes away and won't go back to it. I've seen something in a German magazine showing a dog with a toggle in its mouth, showing that it has found the deer. Can I teach my dog that, or is there a better way of coping with the problem?

The technique you refer to is called the *Bringsel*, and I have a snap of a Labrador which was successfully trained in this complicated idea. It takes a lot of patience! The toggle hangs from the collar and when a dead buck is found, the dog swings the toggle into his mouth, almost as a substitute retrieve, coming back to his handler and then returning to the beast. You can find details in German hunting literature, or if French is easier, in *Le Chien de Sang* by Henri Fuster (Gerfaut Club, ISBN 2-901196-13-6).

Alternatively, you can teach your dog to 'bark dead', staying by the dead beast and barking until you come. If he is used for game shooting as well, this could be an awkward habit, in which case buy either a falconry bell or a small (two to three inches high) tourist cowbell which can be attached to his collar when there is a beast to find. You can usually get there in time before he loses interest in the beast!

I want to train a stalking dog, mainly to be with me, maybe point, but mainly to find deer after the shot as my stalking is in very thick cover. Can you recommend any books or DVDs which would help me, first to decide the best breed and then to give guidance with training?

Three books on the subject of dogs for deer are obtainable through the British Deer Society (www.bds.org). These are:

Guy Wallace, *Training Dogs for Woodland Stalking* (Booklet) 1994 and later editions, Fawley Publications. Guy Wallace is a professional dog trainer who has been involved with deer dogs for many years. Full of practical advice.

Niels Sondergaard, *Working with Dogs for Deer* (www.jagtforlaget.dk). This is a very comprehensive book, very well illustrated and seamlessly translated from Danish.

John Jeanney, *Tracking Dogs for Finding Wounded Deer* (Teckel Time Inc.) 2006 (www.born-to-track.com). Written for the US market, but worth study.

Handling and cooking venison

There is a spot of caveman in most stalkers. We like to pose as the providers, even if the notion of dragging a newly shot beast into the kitchen might not be as welcome these days as it might have been ten thousand years ago. If stalking is to remain an approved activity in your household, the product has to be offered in conveniently sized oven-ready material with a discreet veil drawn over the conversion process.

The younger generation of stalkers will be fully aware of the need to comply with various meat hygiene regulations, but alongside these goes a necessary degree of respect for the quarry and also consideration for the household and neighbours, not all of whom are certain to be sympathetic to field sports. A young friend of mine had a flat above a bath-salts factory in South London. He was interviewed one day by a very suspicious police posse, attracted to the scene of the crime by early-morning comings and goings and a blood smear across the pavement. They assumed the body had been dragged out, not in. Don't be unnecessarily secretive over your stalking activities, but exercise tact.

Venison is a very healthy meat, low in lots of the undesirable elements in the modern diet, but being relatively fat-free it needs sympathetic cooking to keep it moist. The fat itself congeals at a lower temperature than that of beef or lamb, so any dish needs to be served up quickly. Be warned – a constant diet of venison tends to be costive.

Game cookery has become fashionable recently, thanks to a successful campaign and the activities of the TV chefs; however, there are still those who have an objection to eating any wild meat, and I delight in the thought of so many of our guests who having wolfed one helping of venison, have come back for more without realising what was in 'that delicious casserole'.

I haven't too much freezer space at home and a whole roe jointed up won't fit in. I don't want to waste good meat, but would it spoil everything to bone out the lot?

There is a good deal you can do and still produce tasty venison. Certainly bone the shoulders and neck, cutting them up into cubes for casseroling. The fillets can be taken off the backbone (don't forget the delicious little undercut) and either halved or cut into tournedos. You can take the shank bone off each haunch to shorten it, and if necessary carefully cut the meat away from the hip bones down to the point where they articulate with the leg, leaving the main bone in from there to the joint with the shank. If you must bone out the haunch, follow the seams between the big muscles back to where they attach to the bones. Cut up for steaks, or roll and tie with string.

Can I make haggis out of deer offal? It seems a pity to give what seems like promising material to the dogs. It can't be much different from making one from lamb, and I have done that.

I agree that one should make the best use of everything from shot game, and I like haggis too, but there is a snag. Deer fat congeals more quickly than lamb's, so unless the haggis is served very hot, you are likely to get an unpleasantly greasy mouth. I would advise you to try Humble Pie as an alternative, and it is easier to keep piping hot. It used to be made from the liver, kidneys, heart and 'entrails' for the hunt servants after a successful chase. The gentry, of course, ate the haunch and saddle.

Round here a lot of muntjac get knocked over on the roads. They look all right, but are they OK to eat?

It's a temptation, but you need to be aware of the hazards and also to visualise the way in which the animal has died. Quality meat is produced from unstressed animals. This deer was caught crossing the road, and probably panicked before being hit, so the adrenalin will have been pumping into its muscles, changing the pH and thus the palatability of the venison. It is possible that the impact just broke its neck, but more likely there will be extensive bruising before death intervened, plus broken bones etc. Third, it will probably have been dragged some yards along the tarmac, with all the pollutants present being ground into the carcass. No – I don't eat road kills! Nor do I make a tasty stew 'for the beaters' which was recently proposed, to my ultimate horror.

It happened that when your letter arrived I had a game dealer here having some trophies measured, so I asked him his views. What he said was that if you yourself knocked over a deer, and so were able to bleed it quickly, apart from bruised or torn flesh, you could probably salvage the haunches or the saddle. The trouble if you just see a dead deer is to know how long it had been there and whether it died quickly or lingered before dying. In the latter case there would be a change in the pH of the meat, making it taste awful.

If you think of feeding your dogs, well maybe, but be aware that some sympathetic motorist may have seen the beast wounded and has asked a vet to give it a lethal injection. This is more likely to happen to the larger deer species, admittedly, but such cases are on record. In one, a fallow buck was recovered by a stalker in the early morning from a roadside where it had, in fact, been put down in this way though he had no way of knowing. It was taken back to the game larder and dressed out. The stalker's dog ate a bit of the liver and was dead in minutes. Another similar case arose not long ago. So don't eat carrion!

As wild boar are on the increase, how does one prepare such an animal for the larder? I would like to do justice to any quarry I shoot and can see in the early years of the wild boar becoming more common that many carcasses will be mishandled.

- *Is the gralloch much the same as for a deer?*
- *Does one skin it, or boil and shave off the hair?*
- *How long can a wild boar be hung in the larder?*

Your concern for proper treatment of an alien beast is commendable. No doubt as you say, wild boar will spread and become more numerous now they have established themselves, and will make very worthwhile quarry. Farmers with free-range herds of sows have grounds for more worry than has been shown by the authorities to date.

My experience on the Continent is that the gralloch is much the same as for a deer, though one must remember that swine have a gall bladder, missing in deer, which must be removed with care. Apart from that, your training on deer will be a good guide, and of course the sooner the beast is cleaned out and in cold storage the better.

One could truthfully say 'they are pigs to skin', but skinned they have to be. It is a tedious and smelly job, needing repeated resharpening of your knife. If you shoot one in winter coat the cured skin is a fine trophy. I talked to Paul Taylor, the taxidermist, who has experience of skinning boar. He says the skin cannot be pulled, but has to be sliced off. You need a fairly stiff knife and it may be helpful to divide the skin along the spine on the larger animals and take it off in two halves to make the job easier. On an old male the skin is extremely thick and hard over the shoulders. Remember your bullet may have to penetrate this and still go on through!

Like any meat, boar improve with hanging for several days if you have suitable accommodation which must be clean, free of flies, rats and mice or cats and equipped with a chiller to keep the temperature below 7 degrees centigrade. Otherwise, take it to your game dealer and make sure it is in a presentable state for him. Meat from a young boar up to a couple of years old is quite delicious. Older animals could well be strong tasting.

My stalking is mostly for roe and fallow, and the family really appreciate eating venison. There does seem to be quite a difference from one carcass to another, regardless of species. Can you explain this? Is it a matter of age?

As far as my experience goes, much more depends on the respective skills of the stalker and the cook than the age of the beast.

Regarding fallow, or the other large deer species for that matter, the pressures of the rut make venison shot in early autumn better passed to less discriminating households! I was once given a quantity of rutty red venison and no matter how it was cooked, even in chilli-con-carne or curry, it was still strongly reminiscent of the rut. Roe take their rutting activities much less seriously and apart from a slight loss of condition, one can usually get away with it, always remembering that venison is dry meat and needs sympathetic cooking.

The crunch comes in the way a beast is shot and subsequently handled. The best venison comes from a beast which was totally unsuspecting at the time of the shot, and dropped immediately. Alarm immediately leads to a flush of adrenalin and physical changes in the muscles which can be detected in the meat. Similarly, a poor, wounding shot needing follow-up and dispatch seriously affects palatability.

Then there is the matter of bleeding, gralloch and transport. A chest shot can be depended on to lead to extensive internal bleeding which is sufficient, and in most cases a knife in the sticking point of the neck will produce very little blood.

It is important to carry out the gralloch very quickly and to make a clean job of it, not soiling the meat with body contents, and above all, removing the entire digestive tract unpunctured, leaving the space below the aitch-bone completely clear.

Then the carcass needs to be transported quickly to cool, ventilated, fly-free storage. Do this, and you can depend on best-quality venison.

If one is to be particular about age, for my taste I would choose a yearling, winter-fat roe doe, or a fallow pricket shot in August, but this is gourmet stuff compared with the other points I have mentioned.

I can get supplies of venison from our shoot here, but I am not sure what bits to ask for. When I get it, does it have to be hung and then marinated, or what? Please advise.

If you want a nice joint to roast and you are in the Midlands, you can probably get muntjac haunches (back leg) about a couple of kilos, or for a bigger party, a young fallow haunch from a doe or yearling buck. Definitely **not** from a buck near or after the rut, which is likely to be rank. Any hanging, ideally a week or so in cold weather, has to be done before the beast is skinned otherwise the surface of the meat goes dark and hard. All venison freezes well because of the lack of fat.

The saddle (loin) cooked on the bone is delicious, or you can ask for boneless fillets to make small tournedos which do not need much cooking. Steaks are often cut from the muscle of the haunch of larger animals. These may benefit from a light thumping with a steak mallet through a sheet of cling film.

You can marinate if you like, but first-quality venison from a beast which has been well shot and dressed doesn't need more than pepper and salt plus a few crushed herbs to make a gourmet dish.

I hate to throw venison kidneys away or give them to the dogs, but when somebody cooked them for me they were very strong in taste, hard and shrivelled. Is this something I have been missing all these years?

What a waste! My dogs only got a kidney when they were too quick for me!

Obviously the kidneys from a rutting buck or stag can be rank, but otherwise with quite basic treatment roe kidneys especially, are excellent.

If you are going to freeze them, just give them a quick rinse and leave the covering of fat which preserves them. To prepare – split lengthwise and take off various layers of skin, cutting the pipe leading away as close as you can to the kidney. Soak overnight in milk which is discarded before cooking.

They need gentle heat, even when grilling. I cover the kidney halves with a spray of olive oil and a dusting of pepper and paprika. Grill them slowly until just firm then serve either on toast or rice. It is worth keeping the pan juices to pour over, with or without a touch of cream. Delicious!

There is an excellent recipe for kidney marinated and barbecued in that invaluable book *The Venison Cook* by Diane and Nicholas Dalton (Crowood Press).

Is it possible to smoke venison? My household gets a bit tired of continuous roast roebuck, stewed roebuck, veniburgers or curried fallow for a change. If one can smoke pheasants and so on, why not? Is there a book on the subject?

Certainly it is possible to smoke venison, and very good it can be! In various countries, mainly Scandinavian, I have had excellent smoked roe haunch and even smoked elk heart and tongue. Maybe one could do something similar with red deer tongues, but anything smaller might be fiddly. Maro Bregolli, a keen roe stalker, master chef and one-time proprietor of a celebrated restaurant in Romsey had a way of taking two roe fillets, stringing them together into the shape of a fat sausage and, after salting and seasoning, hanging them for a couple of days in the wide chimney of the open fire in his restaurant. This was sliced thinly like salami and was quite memorable.

Venison is a very dry meat, while smoking usually goes best with oily or fatty material, so success may not come immediately. Don't use softwood sawdust – it taints the meat. Oak heartwood is considered best, but beware the sapwood – it may be carcinogenic.

Hot smoking cooks the meat and could work well for small pieces for eating immediately. Cold smoking for larger cuts needs care and if you want to experiment, a reliable book is advisable. Keith Erlandson's, *Home Smoking and Curing* (Bushwear list it at £9.95) has been a standby for years, or they quote another *Home Book of Smoke Cooking Meat, Fish and Game* by Sleight & Hall at £10.95. Bushwear can be contacted at 0845 226 0469.

Help! I've been asked to do a shoot picnic on Christmas Eve, of all times, and need something festive, but which must be done ages before. We have lots of roe bits and pheasants but not much else.

I don't like lukewarm food out of a Thermos. If you have any way of keeping things hot at the lunch place, there is nothing like a venison goulash to warm people who have been out all morning and it can be done and frozen well before. Remember to be lavish with the paprika – the Hungarians told me one should lightly perspire afterwards! With carrots, turnip and onions in it already, they can eat it out of bowls with a spoon and be well fed. There is a good recipe in *The Venison Cook* by Diane and Nicholas Dalton.

For a cold picnic, split pheasant breasts and smear the cut with pesto. Wrap each one with rindless bacon and grill them. These too can be frozen. When cold, cut into roundels and use them to fill wholemeal baps, together with shredded lettuce and mayonnaise.

If you want a starter to hand round and soften the effect of the sloe gin, why not make some venison liver paté? It's very quick to do and freezes well. Just slice some roe liver and cook it gently in plenty of butter till soft. Put it in the food processor with garlic powder, pepper and salt to taste. Get the texture right by adding sherry. We don't include any bacon – you are going to spread it like caviar on small oatcakes or chunks of bread and the bits are difficult to cut and get in the way.

If they want anything else after that, a batch of flapjacks ought to do the trick.

Acknowledgements

Trying to give an answer to stalkers who write in to *Shooting Times & Country Magazine* over the last ten years or so has been a pleasure and at times a real challenge and I am so grateful to you all for providing much of the basic material in this book. You must excuse me for not putting in your names: some would have welcomed it, others not. Also, freed from the constraints of a regular feature, many answers have been extended or combined because inevitably some subjects come up time after time. The difficulty has been to know what to cut out, so with reluctance I have not included those fascinating queries which related to special circumstances or were unlikely to recur. Thanks also for many photos, some of which I have used. Unfortunately tracing the original photographers has not been possible, so this has to be an acknowledgement and an apology.

Tony Jackson has been a friend since my first efforts in journalism and has handled the mass of sometimes hurried and ill-written 'Answers' with unvarying good humour. He has now added to his kindness with a Foreword, for this, my swansong which was compiled at his suggestion. Thanks also to Brian Phipps for permission to use some of his matchless deer portraits.

Nothing would have been possible without permission from the Proprietors of *Shooting Times & Country Magazine* to use material which appeared in their ever-popular journal. Also to Charlie Parkes and John Thornley for similar permission. Their book, *Deer Law*, has been my bible for all those tricky questions which deal with people (who are so much more difficult to manage) rather than with deer only. My thanks to everyone.

Richard Prior

Index